the **BOOK** of

Brownie Skills

Purnell

Contents

Indoors

the **BOOK** of
Brownie Skills

SBN 361 03577 2

Copyright © 1976 Purnell and Sons Limited
Published 1976 by Purnell Books, Berkshire House,
Queen Street, Maidenhead, Berkshire
Made and printed in Great Britain by Purnell and Sons
Limited, Paulton (Bristol) and London
Reprinted 1979, 1981

Outdoors

Indoors

Helping at Home

Let's make no bones about it; household chores are really pretty boring work. Sweeping and dusting; cleaning and polishing; washing and ironing; washing-up and making beds; it's hardly the action of adventure stories. Actually nobody likes doing them, but everybody hates it if they aren't done! The best idea is for everybody to lend a hand so that they all get done as quickly as possible, leaving you free to do more interesting things.

You can always make chore-time more fun by making it into a game, or using it as a time to practise your singing, or to think up an idea for a story. You'll have to concentrate on what you are doing some of the time, though!

Washing-Up

This is a several-times-a-day chore; after each meal and cooking session. It's easier to do immediately after things have been dirtied, rather than when they have been standing for hours.

Stack everything to be washed near the sink in neat piles that are not going to topple over the minute your back is turned. Empty all the dregs down the sink and scrape any bits of food into a sink basket. It makes washing-up even easier if you rinse off the dirty plates first; if they are greasy and sticky, use hot water, but if they have had starchy, fishy, milky or eggy food on them, use cold water. You could soak the cutlery in jam jars of soapy water, too, but don't put bone handles into water; they will soon come off.

Then wash up, and there's even a correct order for washing. It goes: glasses, silver and cutlery, cleanest china, greasy china, kitchen utensils, and pots and pans last.

If you've got lots and lots of washing-up to do, it's best to dry up some of it as you go along, and better still if you do so while the things are still hot from the water. You may need a second bowl of clean, hot soapy water if the first one gets a bit murky!

Put everything away, wash down the draining board and sink, and that's the washing-up dealt with!

Cleaning Silver, Brass and Copper

This is a good chore for singing to while you are rubbing. Remember, the idea is to remove the dirt altogether, not just to transfer it to yourself or the table you are working on.

Collect together all the things that need cleaning; brass fenders and trays, copper coal buckets, kettles and pans, silver dishes and cups, and forks and spoons that have become tarnished. Spread lots of newspaper over the surface where you are working and set to work. Use a commercial metal polish and rub in a small amount at a time, making sure you don't neglect hard-to-get-at corners. Polish up with a soft cloth and lots of elbow grease. It's quite a good idea to wash and dry cutlery after cleaning just to make sure all the polish has gone; it doesn't taste too good!

Did you know that you can tell a lot about the silver things you have just cleaned by reading the marks on them? In 1327 Edward III granted a charter to the Goldsmiths' Guild, allowing them to assess and standardise the quality of all silver articles made in this country. Up until then, and in fact for long after, too, silver arti-

A Complete Hall Mark

MAKER
(Zedd Co Ltd)

STANDARD
(Sterling Silver)

TOWN MARK
(Birmingham)

DATE LETTER
(1951)

cles weren't the valuable and prized possessions they are today. Even during the sixteenth and seventeenth centuries, people thought nothing of melting down old solid silver objects to fashion them into more modern designs, or even to make silver coins to pay off their debts. That is why it is almost impossible to find silver objects from before this time, and why they are correspondingly valuable.

Solid silver objects usually have a tiny row of 'puncheon' marks on them, from which you can tell the name of the maker (indicated by a symbol or an initial), the date it was made (indicated by a letter which is changed in May every year), and where it was made (indicated by various emblems). London has a leopard's head, Birmingham an

STERLING
STANDARD
SILVER

BRITANNIA
STANDARD
SILVER

anchor, and Edinburgh a castle, for example. In addition there is a 'Standard Mark', which is usually a walking lion. This shows that the silver contains the correct amount of fine silver. If there is a figure of Britannia instead, it means the silver contains a higher amount of fine silver. If the object was made between 1784 and 1890, it will also have a sovereign's head, which shows that the duty levied on silver at that time had been paid.

Well—if you've finished examining all your sparkling silver, we'd better get back to some more chores!

Stain Removal

Everybody spills things on themselves from time to time. You'd be positively superhuman if you never got biro or felt-tipped pen streaks on your blouse, or never tipped a cup of tea or coffee into your own or someone else's lap. If stains are treated quickly, they can usually be made to disappear altogether, leaving no embarrassing tell-tale marks as reminders of the incident. Often just a squeezing through of cool water as soon as the damage is done will rid the garment, and memory, of them for ever. All too often, however, it's not too easy to render immediate action, so here are some hints on how to remove stubborn stains.

Wrong side of fabric

Clean part of fabric

Always try to work from the wrong side of the fabric, and hold a dry, clean pad of material behind it to absorb the stain and the damp. Apply the recommended solution outside the perimeter of the stain and work in towards the centre. This way you should avoid getting 'rings' on the fabric. If the fabric is washable, wash it in the normal way after treating it.

Tea and jam—Soak in cold water and borax

Coffee and cocoa—Moisten stain with one part glycerine to two parts water. Soak in cold water

Blood and egg—Soak in cold water and salt

Ink—Put lemon juice or milk and then salts of lemon on the stain and leave for 10 to 15 minutes. Put a damp cloth over stain and iron it. Repeat; rinse; and then wash normally

Crayon (also any greasy or fatty stain)—Use a grease solvent

Biro and felt-tipped pen and grass—Rub with methylated spirit

Chocolate—Scrape off as much as possible. Apply a grease solvent

Ice cream—If stain doesn't come out when washed normally, use a grease solvent

Bed-Making

If the bed is against the wall, pull it out so you can get round it easily. Then pull back the covers and the top sheet and tuck the bottom sheet in all round so it is smooth, taut and unwrinkled. Pull up the top sheet making sure it is tucked in at the bottom of the bed, and then pull up all the blankets, one by one, making sure they are all smooth. If you

11

are a super-one-hundred-per-cent-expert bedmaker, you should really tuck in the top sheet and each blanket separately all the way round! But most people are prepared to relinquish the title and save a little time, instead, by tucking the whole lot in together at the bottom with hospital corners. Then turn over the sheet and the blankets at the top and tuck in neatly along both sides. Plump up the pillow; put it at the top of the bed and pull the bedspread over the lot. Best of all, persuade your family to use duvets; bedmaking is over with one quick shake!

Room Cleaning

If you are cleaning a bedroom, make the bed first. Thereafter the order in which you clean is the same for any room. Empty the wastepaper baskets and put away any clothes, shoes, yesterday's newspapers, and so on. Then dust all the surfaces, starting with the top ones and working downwards. I'm afraid it means moving all those ornaments, alarm clocks, photographs and potted plants, however carefully arranged they are. Sweep the floor, and/or carpet-sweep or vacuum-clean the carpet, including under and behind chairs and tables.

Finally, you can polish the tops of any furniture that needs it (the same rules apply as for cleaning silver and brass; a little polish and lots of elbow grease).

To clean the bath and basin, first remove all the bits of soap, nailbrushes, rubber ducks and so on, and clean all round with a paste cleaner (tiled surrounds as well). Rinse out well afterwards and polish up the taps with a dry cloth.

Things You Should Know

PREVENTING ACCIDENTS IN THE HOME

We talk about road safety on pages 137-42. The reason why we are conscious of road safety is that it helps to prevent accidents. Exactly the same applies in the home, where, amazingly, almost more accidents happen than anywhere else. Nearly all of them can be avoided with nothing more than a little thought. Here are some accident-preventing moves; see if you can think of some more.

1. Never play with unused matches.
2. Keep away from gas stoves and fires.
3. Never eat pills because you think they might taste nice.
4. Never drink liquid from bottles unless you are **absolutely** sure what it is (don't necessarily trust the label!).
5. Never leave anything, especially toys and balls, on the floor or stairs where people can trip over them.
6. If it's dark, always put on the light before going up or down stairs.
7. Don't come downstairs carrying so much that you haven't a free hand, or, worse still, can't see where you are going.

8. Don't stand on a wobbly chair, or table, or on tip-toe to get something off the top of a wardrobe.

9. If you spill anything, particularly something greasy, wipe it up at once. Someone may skid on it.

10. Don't play with electric light switches. Always turn off the current before pulling out or pushing in plugs. Don't touch any electric appliances with wet hands.

11. If you are helping to cook, never leave the oven door open and turn all saucepan handles towards the cooker; don't leave them sticking out beyond it where they may be a temptation to a young child to reach up and pull off. Be extra careful when using sharp knives; always try to cut with the blade pointing away from you.

How many other precautions can you think of to take?

FIRST AID

Accidents happen. Many, it is true, could be avoided; but because—however careful you are—they will occur from time to time, everyone should have some basic knowledge of what to do. This is called 'first aid'

If you are treating someone else who has hurt themselves, remember you should be very calm yourself: be quietly cheerful, so that your patient is reassured. Panic in you promotes panic in other people, and no one gets anywhere—very quickly.

Below we tell you how to deal with such things as minor cuts and grazes, nonserious burns and nosebleeds, but if someone you are with has an accident that you feel unable to cope with, or hurt themselves in such a

way that they need adult or even medical attention, there is a special procedure to follow.

1. Tell an adult or an older person **immediately** that an accident has occurred.

2. If the accident happens at home, and there is no grown-up present, telephone your doctor or ring 999. Say who you are, where the patient is and **briefly** what has happened.

3. If someone has fallen off a ladder, or from a tree during a climbing game, never try to move her to make her 'more comfortable'. She may have some broken bones or internal bleeding which you will make worse. Tell her to keep still and run and get help.

4. Stay with the patient after you've called for help, but be on the look-out all the time for it to arrive.

Don't panic—you have done all you can.

Cuts and Grazes

Wash your hands first with soap and water. Then clean the wound **gently,** using warm water and soap if there's a lot of dirt around it. Use a clean rag or piece of cotton wool. Then cover the wound with a plaster dressing or a bandage to keep it clean.

A tip about plaster dressings
These sometimes seem unwilling to stick, particularly on bending knees and elbows, where they are often most needed! If you cut either end of the sticky part up to the dressing pad and then separate the parts as you place it over the wound, it will help it to stick better.

Bandages: bandages can be used to keep dressings in place and wounds clean. They are useful for ankles, knees and elbows. Put a pad of gauze over the wound and then bandage round it with a cotton bandage, about 5 cm wide. Always bandage from a rolled-up bandage—it's much easier to handle and enables you to keep your bandaging firm and neat. Start a little way away from the wound and overlap each round of bandage, up and over the wound and beyond. Cut the bandage, and then, holding

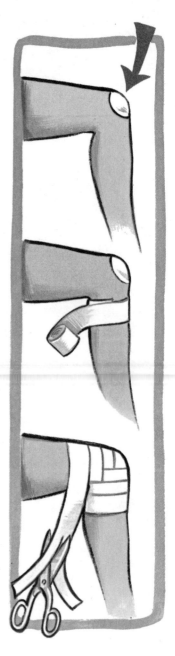

the end, cut down the middle for about 16-20 cm. Tie a knot with these ends against the uncut part of the bandage and then wrap the ends round the leg or arm in opposite directions. Tie securely together with a reef knot to lie flat against the bandage whilst keeping it in place. (Don't tie the knot on top of the injury.)

If you are bandaging a cut on an ankle, start by winding the bandage round the instep of the foot, crossing it up and round the ankle and back under the foot a few times.

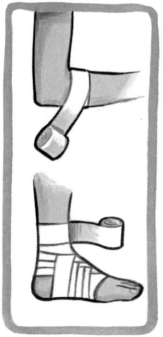

Minor Burns and Scalds

It's very easy to give yourself a nasty burn or scald, so follow these simple precautions! Make sure that you don't touch the hot plates on the electric cooker, or get too near the flames on a gas stove. When you're helping Mother in the kitchen be sure to turn all the saucepan handles or the kettle spout inwards, so that they can't be reached by your young brother or sister. When you help to lay the table turn the tablecloth edges under; then younger members of the family can't pull a hot teapot off the table and scald themselves.

Don't ever play with matches. Open fires should always be covered with a fireguard, preferably a fixed one. Make sure that you don't walk round the house in loose, trailing clothes like your nightie or dressing gown, which can easily catch in a fire—another good reason for getting up and dressed quickly!—and never stand close to an unguarded fire. Some nightdresses, such as those made of flannelette or winceyette, catch fire easily, so see if you can persuade Mother to buy you a flame-proofed or flame-resistant one.

Don't be silly enough to put your hands in water that

17

is far too hot, and it's a good idea to run the cold water before the hot in your bath; then you can only get a frozen and not a scalded foot!

Do you know what to do if someone's clothes catch fire? Immediately wrap a rug, a coat, a tablecloth or any piece of large thick material round the person calling for help. Push her to the ground and roll her over to beat out the flames; (the idea is to smother them because fire can only burn if it has oxygen). If there is literally nothing to hand to wrap round the person, just push her to the ground and roll her over and over to beat out the flames. Get help immediately if none has arrived.

Never try and treat bad burns—always fetch a grown-up. For minor burns, just apply cold water to the affected area. If the burn is on a finger, for example, hold it under a running cold tap for a few minutes.

If the skin has been broken, a doctor should see to it.

Nose Bleeds

Although they look messy and are very uncomfortable, nose bleeds are seldom serious. If your friend (or you) has one, tell her to sit down and tip her head forward a little. Pinch the lower soft part of her nose firmly with your finger and thumb. Hold it for a while (maybe as much as fifteen minutes if it is bleeding badly). She will have to breathe through her mouth, but tell her not to swallow if she can possibly help it. She shouldn't blow her nose for the rest of the day, either.

HEALTHY & HAPPY

You can't be unhealthy and happy! The two just don't mix. Being unhealthy means staying indoors, feeling miserable and sorry for yourself while your 'fit' friends are having lovely fun and games outside.

The First Steps to Health

If you're not clean, you'll never be healthy. In fact the first step to healthiness is keeping clean, and if that sounds a bit boring, don't worry too much, because it is something that will become second nature to you.

Being clean makes a difference to your whole life. Friends don't stay friends with people who look as if they could grow a prize crop of potatoes under their fingernails, who have hair that looks rather like a matted old hearthrug, and who look as if the only thing they ever do with water is drink it!

The Skin-and-Nail Routine

It sometimes seems an awful waste of precious time to take a bath. There are other things you could be doing; but admit it, don't you feel much better after it? Look at it this way—your skin is actually working very hard at trying to keep you healthy, so it seems only fair to help it now and again. Your skin is covered with tiny holes called pores. Through these your body pushes out tiny beads of moisture called perspiration or sweat, which not only help to keep you cool, but also carry in them some of the waste products your body does not want. If you let them stay on your skin, the perspiration dries, but the waste products remain and clog up the pores, helped still further by the dust and dirt in the air. Thus the skin can no longer do its work for you; the waste materials stay in your body, making you dull and lethargic and generally a few degrees under. All you have to do is to help your skin help you by washing it with nice clean water and soap each day.

There's a cautionary tale about a little boy called Struwelpeter who never cut his nails (he didn't look after his hair either, come to that!). He came to a nasty end; so don't be a Struwelpeter yourself. Keep your nails short by cutting them with nail scissors or filing them with an emery board, not by biting them. This horrid habit ruins the shape of your nails for ever; you will never be able to have elegant fingernails when you grow up. Anyway, there are lots of things that taste an awful lot better than bitten nails! Keep your nails clean by scrubbing regularly with a nailbrush.

The Teeth-and-Hair Routine
Would you put away the spoons and forks you have used without washing them

first? Of course not, so don't go to bed without brushing your teeth first! Brushing them in the morning, after you've had breakfast, means they start the day off clean,

too, and if you can rinse them round with water after other meals, so much the better. It all helps to get rid of those particles of food, like the ones on your knives and forks. If you don't look

after your teeth well, you'll be seeing much more of the dentist than you will want to.

Beautiful shining hair everybody can have, whether they are blonde or brunette, have curly, straight, short or long hair. It's just a matter of shampooing it, probably once a week, unless you have very greasy hair. Keep it well brushed and combed, free from tangles, and have it well cut in a style that suits you. Don't forget to wash your brush and comb, too, otherwise it will be like sweeping a clean floor with a dust-laden broom. A pretty futile practice!

KEEPING FIT WITH YOGA EXERCISES

As we have seen, happiness and healthiness go hand-in-hand. And you're not really healthy unless you're fit. So being 'fit' is obviously a good thing if you want to lead a happy life!

As well as being in good physical condition, keeping fit means learning to relax. A dictionary definition of 'fit' is 'to be the right size and shape for. . .'. And that is just what you want to be; the right size and shape for enjoying life and living it to its full, both mentally and physically.

Yoga is a beautiful way of keeping fit at the same time as teaching you to relax, the perfect combination. Thousands of years ago some people called 'Yogis' devoted their whole life to practising yoga in all its many forms, and people have been following yoga teachings and practices ever since. The fact that it is still widely practised throughout the world today says quite a lot for it!

Yoga involves no violent exercise; in fact it is done in a calm, fluent way and the exercises are designed to exercise *every* part of your body. To go into it fully is way beyond the scope of this book, but it is an extremely interesting subject which you may like to study further on your own.

There are a few yoga exercises on the following

what you are doing. If you are going to fit them in in a spare few minutes before dashing off to do something else, you might as well not bother, because they won't do you any good at all that way.

3. Breathe evenly, regularly and normally while you are doing the exercises; (you're not supposed to be over-exerting yourself, remember). Hold each position as you achieve it before return-

pages which will help you to feel fitter and better. Whenever you do them remember that:

1. You should never strain yourself. Only do as much as you can each time, and as you practise more you will be able to do each exercise a little better each time.

2. Always be quiet and relaxed when you do your exercises. Put aside at least fifteen minutes for each session and think only about

ing, slowly, to normal.

4. Don't do yoga exercises for at least two hours after you've had a meal.

Exercises

Relax! This sounds like the easiest exercise of all, because what you do is just lie flat on your back on the floor! In fact to do it properly is very hard. Lie really, really flat so that even the hollow of your back is touching the floor. Your legs should be outstretched, your ankles so relaxed your feet flop over towards the floor. Let your arms stretch out beside you in the most comfortable place, with your palms facing upwards. Now think about nothing; not what you have been doing during the day, not about what you may be having for tea; nothing. Let your mind go quite blank and aim at relaxing every muscle in your body. If a friend picks up one of your hands, for example, it should just flop back down to the floor when she lets go.

Shoulder-Stand. Why not give your feet a rest and stand on your shoulders for a change? It's good for your brain, too, because it gets an unusual flow of good, restorative blood rushing to it. In addition it really stretches the muscles of your legs, back, abdomen, neck and spine. Lie on your back on the floor, with your arms by the side of your body and your palms flat on the ground. Slowly raise your legs, keeping them together until they are sticking straight up in the air. Put your hands on your hips and

then raise your hips and your body, too, until only your head and shoulders are on the floor, with your body in a straight line above them. Stay like that for a minute or two before lowering your body and legs slowly back to the ground.

Cat-Stretch. Have you ever watched a cat getting up after a sleep? Slowly and luxuriously it arches its head and back, then it stretches each of its legs in turn; even its tail quivers as those muscles are exercised. There's an exercise called the Yoga Cat Stretch, which stretches all your muscles in the same way. Kneel on the floor and put your hands on the ground in front of you. Drop your head down between your arms and push your back up in the air, just like the cat. As you lower your back, stretch your head up to pull the neck muscles. Finally raise each of your legs in turn as high into the air as you can. Think of being a cat. Think of your muscles and feel them stre- . . . e . . . e . . . tching.

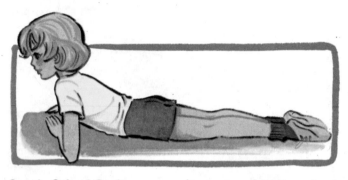

Supple-Spined Snake.

When a cobra is about to strike, it rears its body up in the air. Just think of how supple its spine must be to do that. Then see how supple yours is. Lie on the floor on your tummy with your hands tucked in front of your chest, almost under your chin, in fact. Slowly make your head and shoulders rise in the air. Then rise up from your waist, your spine curving gently, with your arms outstretched in front of you and your palms flat on the floor. Hold the position for a few minutes (are you thinking about being a snake?), then slowly

return to your lying position on the floor.

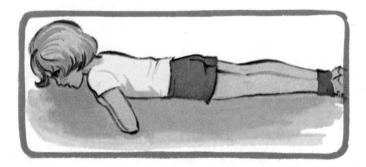

Handicrafts

KNITTING

Knitting is one of the most useful things to know how to do. You can make all sorts of lovely things when you know how to knit—from clothes for you, your friends or your dolls' family (even dolls themselves!), to household items such as mats, egg-cosies and cushion covers, all of which make super presents. One of the best things about knitting is that you can pick it up and do it whenever you have a few odd moments to spare. Once you've begun something you don't have to carry on with it until it is finished. That's why you can always have a piece of knitting on the go.

Remember, when you first learn to knit you will find it very difficult—even to do at all. But keep practising and suddenly you will find you have become quite an expert without realising it!

There are four basic steps to master in knitting:

1. Casting on stitches
2. Knitting plain (or gar-

ter) stitch
3. Knitting purl stitch
4. Casting off stitches

Once you can do these, and have learnt how to read knitting patterns, you can knit almost anything! And all you need to start is a pair of knitting needles and a ball of wool.

To cast on

1. Make a loop near the end of the ball of wool and slip it onto a needle. Hold this needle in your left hand.

4. Slip the loop you have made onto the left-hand needle. Make more stitches in the same way.

2. Push the point of the other needle through the loop and wind the wool once round the needle.

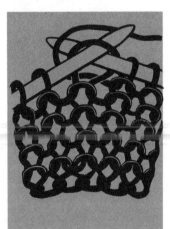

3. Pull this needle and wool through the first loop, so you now have a loop on each needle.

To knit plain or garter stitch

1. With a row of stitches on the left-hand needle, push the point of the other needle into the front of the first stitch and wind the wool round.

2. Draw the needle through the stitch and then slip the stitch off the left-hand needle. Continue in this way to the end of the row.

hand needle lift the *first* stitch you knitted over the second one and drop it off the needle.

3. Knit one more stitch and repeat the process, continuing to the end of the row.

To knit purl stitch
1. With a row of stitches on the left-hand needle, push the point of the other needle into the front of the first stitch, but this time keep it in *front* of the work.
2. With the wool also in front, wind it once over the top of the needle. Draw the needle through the stitch and slip the stitch off the needle. Continue to the end of the row.

If you knit every row in a piece of knitting in plain or garter stitch, your knitting will look the same from both sides—and will have even rows of slightly raised loops.

To cast off
1. Knit two stitches onto the right-hand needle.
2. With the point of the left-

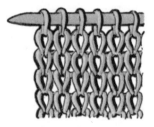

If you knit one row of plain stitch, and then one row of purl stitch, you will have worked 'stocking stitch', which is smooth on one side with close rows of loops on the other side.

If you knit a row of one stitch in plain, followed by one stitch in purl, you will have knitted in 'rib'. This makes the knitting look narrower because it gives it some natural elasticity.

Even if the first thing you are going to knit is something very simple, like squares for a blanket or a scarf, practise all these basic steps first until you can really do them well.

A warm woolly scarf
Just the thing for cold, blustery days. Make it for yourself or as a present for a friend.

You will need:
3 25-gramme balls of double knitting wool in yellow
3 25-gramme balls of double knitting wool in blue
1 pair No. 8 knitting needles
Darning needle

How to make the scarf:
Cast on 38 stitches. Knit your scarf in knit 2, purl 2 rib, as this will make it firm and thick. Knit 12 rows in each colour, breaking the wool off at the end of each block and leaving a length of at least 10 cm. Keep some wool back for the fringe at either end, and then just knit until you run out of wool! Cast off. Your scarf will be a little over a metre long—which is an ideal length!

Thread each of the loose ends along the side of the scarf onto a darning needle and sew them neatly along the edge. Then run the needle 1 cm into the knitting and cut off the end very close to the work.

Tassels on either end will make your scarf look really professional. Cut the wool you have saved into 10-cm lengths. Fold each one of these in half and thread the double thickness through a darning needle. Starting at one side, thread each strand through the cast-off edge. Slip the needle off the wool and thread the cut ends of the wool through the loop. Pull firmly to secure the tassel. Repeat along both cast-off edges, keeping the tassels close together.

Knitting Patterns

When you begin to knit from printed knitting patterns you will find the instructions are written in an abbreviated way which you must learn to follow. These are the abbreviations you need to know.

K=knit (plain stitch)
P=purl
st(s)=stitch (stitches)
st. st.=stocking stitch
inc=increase stitches
dec=decrease stitches
K 2 tog=knit 2 stitches together
beg=beginning
cont=continue
alt=alternate
bet=between
rep * to *=repeat instructions given between asterisks
r(s)=row (rows)
n.r.=next row

To make the mittens (see next column), which will make a lovely set with the scarf, you will need to be able to follow the abbreviations, and you will also need to know how to increase and decrease stitches.

To decrease stitches
This is the easiest of all! Simply knit (or purl) two stitches together.

To increase stitches
Knit (or purl) a stitch in the ordinary way, but before slipping it off the needle, knit (or purl) again into the back of the loop so you make an extra stitch.

Winter mittens
You will need:
1 25-gramme ball of double

knitting wool in yellow
3 25-gramme balls of double knitting wool in blue
1 pair No. 8 knitting needles
1 pair No. 10 knitting needles
Darning needle

How to make the mittens:
Backs (knit 2 pieces both the same)
With yellow wool, and using No. 10 needles, cast on 24 sts. Work K2, P2 rib for 5 cm. Break wool and change to st. st. using blue wool and No. 8 needles. Begin with a K r. *K4 sts and inc into next st*. Rep from * to * 3 times more so you have 28 sts. K 30 rs on these sts ending with a P r. To shape the top, dec 1 st at both ends of next r. P 1 r. Dec 1 st at both ends of next 8 rs. Cast off remaining 10 sts.

Palms (knit 2 pieces both the same)
With yellow wool, and using No. 10 needles, cast on 20 sts. Work in K2, P2 rib for 5 cm. Break wool and change to st. st. using blue wool and No. 8 needles. Begin with a K r. *K4 sts and inc into next st*. Rep from * to * 3 more times so you have 24 sts. K 32 more rs on these sts ending with a P r. To shape the top, dec 1 st at both ends of next r. P 1 r. Dec 1 st at both ends of next 6 rs. Cast off remaining 10 sts.

Thumbs—fronts (knit 2 pieces both the same)
With blue wool, and No. 8 needles, cast on 2 sts. In st. st. K 1 r. Inc 1 st at end of next and every following P r, 6 times, so you have 9 sts. Work 13 rs. Dec 1 st at both ends of next 3 rs. P 1 r. Dec 1 st at beg of next r. Cast off remaining 2 sts.

Thumb—backs (knit 2 pieces both the same)
With blue wool, and No. 8 needles, cast on 3 sts. In st. st. and beg with a P r, inc 1 st at the end of next and every following K r, 6 times, so you have 9 sts. Work 13 rs. Dec 1 st at beg of next r. Cast off remaining 2 sts.

To make up the mittens:
Press each piece with a warm iron on the wrong side, but do not press the ribbing as it will flatten it. Sew in any loose ends of wool. With small oversewing stitches (see page 46), sew the diagonally shaped end of each thumb piece to the appropriate back and palm piece, approximately 3 cm above the top of the ribbing. Place the corresponding backs and palms together, right sides inside, and oversew right round the edge (except for the bottom edge, of course!). Turn mittens to the right side.

CROCHET

In many ways crochet has the same basic principles as knitting, in that you start from a ball of wool and by making various stitches you turn it into something to wear or use or play with! The difference is that instead of using knitting needles you use just one crochet hook.

The equivalent of casting on in knitting is to make a chain in crochet.

To make a chain:
1. Make a loop near the end of the wool. Using the hook, pull the wool through to make a slip knot and leave this loop on the hook.

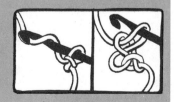

2. Hold the crochet hook between the thumb and index finger of your left hand with the wool looped over the index finger of your left hand.

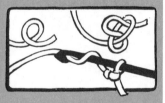

3. Twist wool once round the hook. Hold the slip knot with your left hand and pull the hook with the wool round it through the loop to make a new stitch.

4. Just continue like this until you have a long enough chain.

Now you can learn how to do double crochet stitch.

1. When you have worked a chain, push the hook under the double strands of the *second* stitch from the hook (not counting the loop on the hook). Twist wool once round the hook and pull it through to make a new stitch.

2. Now you have two loops on the hook. Put the wool round the hook again and pull this through both loops, so you have just one stitch on the hook. This completes one double chain stitch.

3. Make double chain stitches into every stitch in the row, and at the end of the chain make one extra stitch.

4. Turn the wool round and work back along the row, taking double chain stitches into every stitch, starting with the last stitch you made on the previous row.

To finish off:
At the end of the final row, just break off the wool and pull it through the loop on the hook.

Crochet bag
You can make this useful bag as soon as you have mastered double crochet stitch.

You will need:
4 50-gramme balls of chunky knitting wool
1 50-gramme ball of chunky knitting wool in a contrasting colour
4 mm crochet hook
Sewing thread
Darning needle
2 press studs

How to make the bag:
Make a chain 26 stitches long. Work in double crochet stitch (remembering the extra chain stitch at the end of each row) until the work is 50 cm long.

Make a thick plait 120 cm long, using the contrasting colour wool. (Don't use quite all the wool.) Tie both ends of the plait securely, leaving a tassel about 5 cm long.

Fold up 20 cm of the bag strip and oversew (see page 46) the edges together. The extra 10 cm makes the flapover. Sew a press stud on both sides of the underneath of this flap and sew the other part of the press stud onto the bag to correspond.

Sew the plait to either side of the bag to make a shoulder strap. Place the bottom of the plait in line with the bottom of the bag so the tassel hangs below it.

Make two chains in the contrasting colour wool and sew them on the flap of the bag in the shape of your initials (the length of the chain will depend slightly on the letters you want to make. Experiment to find out how long they should be).

Besides using double crochet to make straight strips such as the one used in making the bag, you can also work it into circles as you go along.

1. Make a chain of about four to six stitches. Push the hook through the first stitch of the chain and take a stitch. The chain is now formed into a circle.

2. Work about eight or ten double chain stitches round the circle to increase it and bring you back to the starting point.

3. Take a slip stitch to join it to the beginning of the circle and make the end of the circle with a coloured thread.

4. For the next few rounds work two stitches into every other stitch to increase the circle and keep it flat.

5. Thereafter increase one stitch into every third stitch or so. After you have done about seven or eight rounds you don't need to increase stitches for the next few rounds, but should keep your stitches fairly loose so that the circle keeps flat.

A set of table mats
Make a set of table mats following the instructions for crocheting circles and using strong, washable yarn. Make the place mats about 20 cm in diameter,

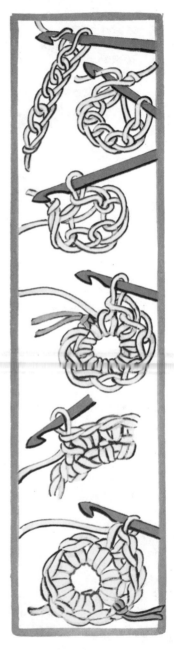

glass coasters about 10 cm in diameter, and a large serving mat about 25 cm in diameter.

A beret

You could also make a beret to match your knitted scarf and mitten set.

You will need:
1 50-gramme ball of double knitting wool in each colour used for the scarf and mittens
4.50 mm crochet hook
Piece of elastic
Darning needle
Cardboard

How to make the beret:
Crochet a circle in stripes of two colours. You will need to crochet about twenty rounds altogether. Sew all loose ends of wool into the wrong side of the work. Then turn a 1-cm hem to the wrong side and sew down, using hem stitch (see page 45). Leave 2 cm unstitched.

Cut a piece of elastic to fit comfortably round your head, allowing an extra 2 cm. Attach one end to a safety pin and make a knot in the other end. Thread the elastic round the circle through the hem. Undo the safety pin and sew the two ends of elastic together firmly. Finish stitching the hem.

Make a pompom to go on

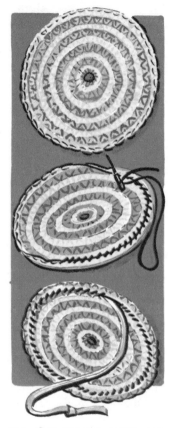

top. Cut out two cardboard circles about 7 cm in diameter. Cut out a circle in the middle of each so you have two rings. Place these together. Thread a needle with both colours of the wool and wind them round and round the rings through the centre hole until it is quite full up. Cut off the ends of the wool, and then cut through the wool at the edge of the rings, using

37

sharp-pointed scissors. Tie a piece of wool between the rings very tightly and then cut the cardboard away. You will be left with a woolly pompom. Trim any straggly ends with the scissors and then sew it to the centre of your beret (on the outside). If you sew it through a little button on the inside of the beret, the pompom will be doubly secure.

WEAVING

Weaving is a very versatile craft and one that anybody can do. It consists of a series of parallel threads called the warp threads across which another series of parallel threads called the *weft* threads are woven. It's a simple idea, and yet, by using different materials—wool, raffia, string, ribbon, beads threaded on strong thread, even strips of fabric—you can achieve a mass of different effects and make any number of different things.

For some weaving you need a loom, and on the next page we show you how to make a couple of simple ones. But there are lots of things you can weave with-

out a loom; how about a set of brightly coloured napkin rings for your family? You can use up odd scraps of wool to make these.

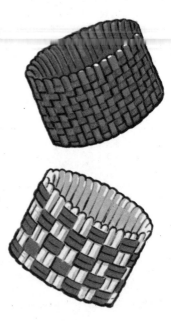

Woven napkin rings

You will need:

Thick cardboard

Glue

Scraps of wool

Darning needle

How to make the rings:

1. Cut the card into strips 15×4 cm. Put glue on the short ends and stick them together to make rings.

2. Wind wool round and round the rings, keeping the strands close together. Thread the end of the wool onto the needle and slip it through the strands to secure it.

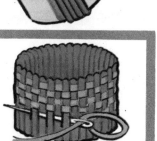

3. Thread the needle with a contrasting colour wool and, starting at the edge, weave in and out of the vertical strands, keeping the rows close together.

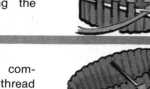

4. When you have completed the weaving, thread the loose ends behind the weaving to finish. Cut off any surplus wool.

5. Weave each ring in a different colour. Try weaving some using a double thickness of wool and taking it over and under two of the vertical threads at a time.

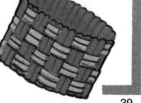

Most flat items are easiest to weave using a loom, as this keeps the warp threads evenly spaced and taut. Here are two simple looms to make.

1. Cut the sides out of a strong cardboard box, approximately 30×20 cm. Cut notches at 1-cm intervals along the ends.

2. Or glue a strip of wood to either end of a piece of strong card or chipboard (again about 30×20 cm). Hammer in small nails at 1-cm intervals along the strips.

1. To thread loom 1, tie a long piece of thread round a notch at one side. Then wind it round and round the box, securing it through the notches.

2. To thread loom 2, tie the thread to an outside nail and wind it round the box between the nails. In both cases wind an extra thread at either side to strengthen the sides of the weaving.

Now use your loom to make a set of table mats—neat partners to your napkin rings.

Table mats
  You will need:
  (to make four mats approximately 25×20 cm)
  Approx. 16 skeins raffia

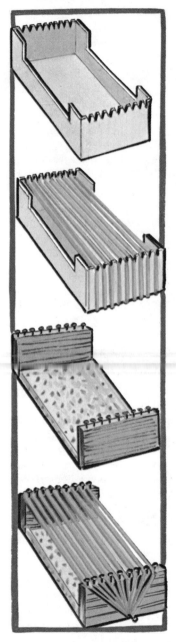

or Raffene (synthetic raffia available in different colours)
Loom (as constructed from instructions)
Raffia needle

How to make the mats:
1. Thread the loom with the raffia to make warp threads.
2. Thread the needle with a length of raffia and, starting at one end, take the weft thread across the warp threads, weaving over one strand and under the next.
3. Weave back across the threads so that the warp thread lies beneath those weft threads it was on top of in the previous row.
4. Continue in this way until you reach the end of the loom. Start each new length of raffia at the beginning of a row.
5. Weave all loose ends into the work (following the pattern) and cut off close to the surface.
6. Turn the loom over and cut off the weft threads to free the weaving. Trim them evenly to make a fringe 2 cm long.
Weave three more mats in the same way.

Now use your imagination to weave other things. Use your loom to weave belts, bags and purses. You can also make bead necklaces

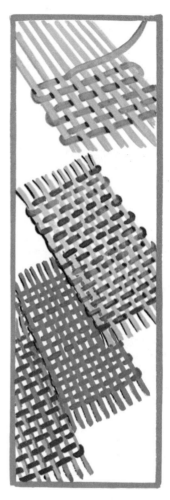

and bracelets on it. Try your hand at paper weaving and make some unusual greetings cards.

SEWING

The basic principles of sewing are less easily explained than those of knitting, crochet or weaving, as there are countless different stitches and sewing techniques, and countless ways of putting them into effect to create sewn articles. However, you can begin to make things as soon as you have mastered just a few stitches and techniques.

The first thing you must do when you learn to sew is to collect together the really essential equipment. There is nothing more annoying than beginning something only to find yourself unable to finish it because you are without a particular needle or type of cotton.

Find a spare clean box or tin or basket and keep all your sewing equipment in it, so that you know exactly where it all is when you want it.

You should have:
A box of pins—always use the rustless kind. Glassheaded ones are pretty and easy to use, but cost a little more than ordinary ones; at least one packet of assorted needles suitable for use on all types of fabric; in addition you need a darning needle, a tapestry needle for canvas embroidery and a crewel needle for other kinds of embroidery; assorted colours and thicknesses of sewing and embroidery thread, plus a reel of tacking cotton which is cheaper than other thread; begin with just a few colours—you will find you soon add to the collection; a tape measure—the fibreglass ones are best; two pairs of scissors—one small pair with sharp points and a larger pair for cutting fabric.

A few sewing hints
Sewing requires a lot of patience and practice, so don't get upset if you don't produce a masterpiece first

42

time. You really will get better the more you do. Also remember that some things will take longer to make than others, so don't get impatient when you seem to have worked for hours without getting much further forward.

 Always make sure your hands are clean before you start to sew. Dirty fingermarks will ruin your sewing quicker than anything, which would be a pity after all that hard work!

When you are not actually doing it, put your sewing away in a polythene bag, or wrap it up in a piece of clean sheeting, so that it doesn't pick up dust and general grime.

Remember to put your sewing equipment away each time you have finished using it. Be particularly careful not to leave pins and needles and scissors lying around, as they could hurt somebody. And while on that subject—be very careful yourself when you are using these things.

✻ Always tack two pieces of fabric together before attempting to sew them with firmer stitches. Don't rely on just pinning them together —pins rarely hold material firmly enough in place.

✻ When you make mistakes—and you will—don't abandon your sewing, casting it aside forever in disgust, however tempted you may be to do so! Instead unpick the mistake and start again—and again, if necessary!

Happy sewing!

Useful stitches
Tacking

Tacking is used to hold two or more pieces of fabric firmly together, or in place, before more permanent sewing is done. It is never left in the finished work. Thread a needle and knot the end. Work from right to left, taking stitches about 1 cm long through all thicknesses of fabric. Keep the needle level all the time. Finish off by going back over the last stitch. Cut the thread.

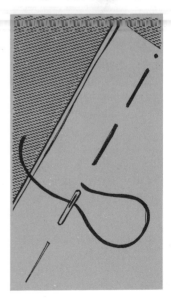

Running stitch
This can be used to hold two

pieces of fabric together permanently.

Work from right to left and take very small (about 2 mm) even stitches. Finish off by going back over the last two stitches.

Back stitch
Back stitch is also used to hold pieces of fabric together and is still firmer than running stitch.

Take two running stitches through the fabric. Then take the needle back to the end of the first stitch and bring it out a stitch length in front. Take the needle back to the end of the second stitch and repeat the process.

Hemming stitch
This is used to hold hems in place at the edge of a garment or item. The stitches should show as little as possible on the right side of the fabric.

Fold the fabric at the hem edge under twice to the wrong side so you have a fold to work along. Keep this in place with a line of tacking. Bring the needle out through the fold so the knot is hidden inside. From right to left, take a small stitch through the fabric beneath the hem and then take the needle back up through the fold. Take another stitch

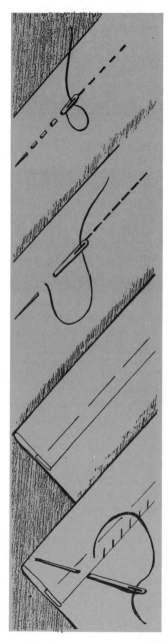

through the bottom fabric and continue in this way to the end of the hem.

Oversewing

This is useful for neatening raw edges or holding two pieces of fabric together at the very edge, when it doesn't matter if the stitches show.

Working from right to left, bring the needle through to the front of the fabric. Take the thread over the top of both pieces of fabric and bring the needle through to the front again so you have made a small slanting stitch. Continue like this.

The following stitches are all embroidery stitches, although they can be used in practical ways as well.

Blanket stitch

This is an attractive stitch to use for neatening raw edges. Work from left to right. Bring the needle through to the front of the work about 4 mm up from the edge. Put it back in about 4 mm farther on, bringing the point out at the edge of the work and making sure that the thread is looped under the needle. Repeat.

Cross stitch

The important thing about

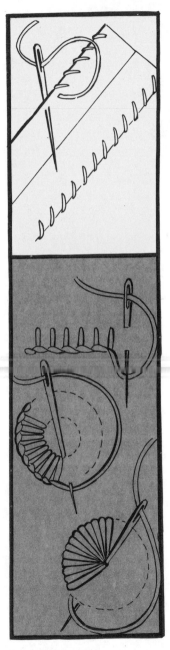

46

cross stitch is to make sure
your stitches are really even.

Work following the diagram. Bring the needle out at
1, put it in at 2, bring it out at
3, put it in at 4 and bring it
out at 3, which now becomes number 1.

Stem stitch
Bring the needle through to
the front of the work. Take a
stitch a little farther on, putting the needle in on the
pattern line and bringing it
out fractionally higher up.

Chain stitch
Bring the needle through to
the front of the fabric. Put it
in next to this point and
bring it out a little farther on,
looping the thread under the
point of the needle. Make
the next stitch in the same
way, putting the needle into
the fabric inside the loop.

Herringbone stitch
You can use this as a
decorative stitch for hems.
Follow the diagram. Bring
the needle out at 1, put it in
at 2, bring it out at 3, put it in
at 4 and bring it out at 1a.
Repeat the process.

An embroidery and felt picture
You will need:
Embroidery canvas
approx. 25×20 cm.

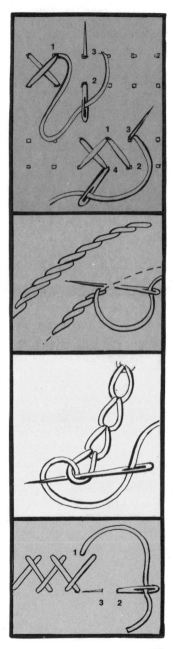

Scraps of yellow, brown and purple felt
Blue ric rac braid
Yellow, brown, red, green, blue and white embroidery threads

How to make the picture:

1. Cut the sand, palm tree trunk, boat and sails from scraps of yellow, brown and purple felt.

2. Sew sand and tree trunk in place with small running stitches.

3. Sew ric-rac waves and boat in place with small running stitches.

4. Embroider the mast in back stitch and top with a cross-stitch flag. Sew sails in place and embroider a herringbone trim on the boat.

5. Sew palm tree trunk in place and embroider large palm fronds with stem stitch.

6. Embroider sun in chain and back stitch. Embroider chain-stitch pebbles on the sand and back-stitch birds in the sky.

7. Edge the picture with a border of blanket stitch.

Cross-stitch gingham apron

You will need:
½ metre checked gingham
Matching sewing thread
Embroidery threads in contrasting colour

How to make the apron:
1. Cut a 12×100-cm strip (for the waistband) and two 14 cm squares (for pockets) from the gingham. Neaten the remaining piece to a rectangle 86×38 cm.
2. Sew two lines of running stitch close to one long edge, leaving a long length of thread at one end. Make hems round the two short sides and remaining long edge, and herringbone in place with coloured thread.
3. Work the cross-stitch dog and flower motif on each of the 14 cm squares. Use the checks to help keep the stitches even. Work plant stem and leaves in stem stitch.
4. Turn under a hem on all four edges of both squares. Hem stitch the top hem, then place pockets on apron front, evenly spaced. Tack in

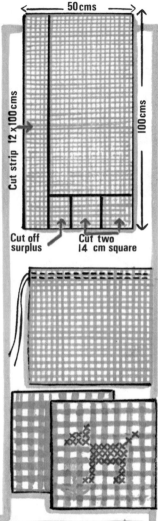

50 cms

100 cms

Cut strip 12 × 100 cms

Cut off surplus

Cut two 14 cm square

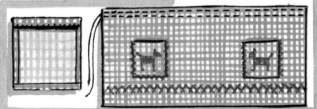

place and then herringbone along the sides and bottom.

5. Iron the band in half lengthways. Pull up running threads on apron to form gathers until edge measures 35 cm. With right sides and edges together, centre the apron on the long strip and tack in place.

6. Back stitch apron to band. Turn under a single hem on the other edge of the band and hem to the back of the apron along the line of the back stitch. Turn under single hems on the sides of the band and oversew together.

7. Work a cross-stitch motif along the band.

Bright patchwork ball

Patchwork is a very attractive form of sewing and is fun and easy to do. It consists of sewing together scraps of fabric, usually cut into regular shapes, and it can be used to make all manner of things. Make this bright ball out of felt, which

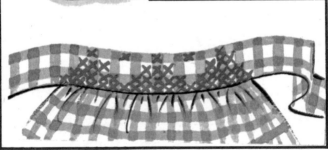

is easy to sew as it does not fray.

You will need:

Tracing paper

Scraps of coloured felt

Embroidery thread

Scraps of fabric for stuffing

25-cm length of ribbon

How to make the ball:

1. Trace off the shape given here and cut it out. Pin it to a piece of felt and cut carefully round the edge. Repeat seven times, using different coloured felt, so you have eight shapes altogether.

2. Sew the pieces together along the long edges with oversewing stitches, using embroidery thread.

3. When you have one seam left, stuff the ball with the scraps of stuffing so that it is a nice round shape.

4. Oversew the last seam to within 2 cm of one end. Fold the ribbon in half and push the ends into the open seam (at the top of the ball). Stitch firmly in place and finish sewing the seam.

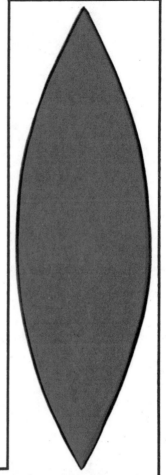

Seasonal Things to Make

The seasons of the year, with their different festivities and celebrations, bring with them some marvellous opportunities for individual creative expression. There are greetings cards you can make for all occasions, presents and decorations to make, special food to cook and so on.

Remember that any gift or card you make yourself will be infinitely more exciting to receive than one you have just gone to a shop and bought.

GREETINGS CARDS

There are lots of different ways of making greetings cards. You can draw and paint a picture; you could use some of the printing ideas on pages 96-101 to print a design; you could glue a pretty arrangement of pressed flowers onto a card; you could cut out pictures from magazines or make a picture by gluing bits of fabric or paper into a pattern. Once you get into the way of making your own cards, you will be able to think up lots of other ideas as well.

Here is a basic list of materials you need to make greetings cards. Add to it according to the card you are making.

Thick paper (cartridge paper is best)
Scissors
Glue
Paints or felt-tip pens
A few extras might be:
Printing materials (pota-

toes, leaves, etc.)
Card for stencils
Oddments of felt and other fabrics
Pages from magazines
Coloured paper
Pressed flowers

As you plan your cards, bear in mind the size of the envelope you intend to use. Nothing is more infuriating than to spend a long time making a beautiful card, only to find it is a couple of centimetres too big for the envelope!

Christmas Cards

Christmas is the time when everybody sends cards, so let's start with some Christmas card ideas. (You could adapt these ideas to make cards for any occasion, though.)

Stencil cards

Stencils used with gold and silver spray paint are particularly good for Christmas cards, especially as it is a good way of making several cards quite quickly.

Draw a fairly large Christmas 'symbol' on a piece of card. Make it something with a simple outline such as a star, a Christmas tree in a pot or an angel shape. Cut out the inside part of the shape to make a stencil. Fold cartridge paper (coloured looks best) to make a card, cover the front with the stencil and either spray on the paint or apply it with a wide-bristled brush.

Snowman card

Draw a snowman shape, like the one shown, onto a piece of card and cut out round the outline. Fold white cartridge paper into a card and place the top of the snowman's hat on the fold. Then draw round him and cut out the snowman shape through both thicknesses of paper (except at the fold). You will have a card in the shape of a snowman, with the fold coming at the top instead of the side. Paint in the details.

Glitter cards

Buy some 'Christmas glitter' which is available in the shops at that time of year.

Fold some black cartridge paper into a card. Draw the outline of two or three lighted candles on the front (don't forget the flame) and then paint in the shape, using a light coating of paper glue. Sprinkle the glitter on the surface of the paper. Leave to dry, then shake off the excess. You will be left with glittery candles. (You'll have to write your Christmas message inside in white paint so it shows up on the black background.)

Easter Cards

Felt chicken

On a piece of thin paper draw and cut out a chicken sitting in a nest or basket, like the one shown. Separate the chicken and the basket by cutting them apart, and use these bits as pattern pieces to cut out a chicken in yellow felt and a basket in brown felt. Fold cartridge paper into a card and glue the chicken sitting in her nest to the front. Cut some 'blades of grass' from green felt and glue these to the background.

Easter egg card

Draw a large egg shape with a bow on top. Put the 'blunt end' against the fold of the card, draw around the outline and cut out (except for the part that touches the fold). Paint the egg and ribbon in bright colours, using paint or felt-tip pens.

Pressed Flower Cards

You will need a selection of pressed flowers for these pretty cards which are useful throughout the year, to thank someone for a party or a gift, to cheer up some-

one who is ill, or just to let somebody know you are thinking of them. (See page 136 for instructions on pressing flowers.)

Fold cartridge paper into a card and arrange your pressed flowers in a design on the front. When you are satisfied with the design, remove the flowers and apply *tiny* smears of glue to the back of the flower and leaf centres. There is no need to put glue on every leaf or petal, just a dot here and there is all that is needed. Put tiny spots at intervals down the stalks and press the flowers very gently into the position in which you want them. When you have stuck down all the flowers, cover the whole surface of the card with self-adhesive transparent cellophane, smoothing it down well to avoid getting any air bubbles on the surface.

Another way of making a pressed flower card is to keep the design in the centre of the card. Then cut out a border in a contrasting colour paper, the same outside size as the card. Stick cellophane over the 'window' in the border, attaching it to the wrong side of the paper. Then glue the border to the front of the card, so that the flower design is framed.

A Good-Luck Card

Fold paper into a card and draw the shape of a horseshoe on the front. Insert the point of your scissors into the shape and cut the inside part away, so you have a cutout horseshoe shape on the front of the card. Trace the outline through to the inside of the card and paint in the outline and details, such as the nail holes, on the inside of the card. Write the words GOOD LUCK on the front of the card beneath the horseshoe or else cut these letters from the pages of an old magazine and paste them down. Then, just for good measure, draw and paint in a little black cat inside the horseshoe shape, on the front of the card.

day cards for special people, drawing or making a picture that means something personal and special to them; make bon voyage cards for friends going on a journey by cutting out a picture of a car or a ship or an aeroplane (depending on how your friends are travelling) and gluing it to a card. Try cutting out different shapes on the front of the card (like the horseshoe in the good luck card) and drawing or gluing a picture on the inside of

These should give you some thoughts and ideas for making cards—so adapt them to make cards for other occasions. Experiment with having the fold of the card at the top instead of the side, like the snowman card, or try folding the paper concertina fashion and write your message right across the whole card.

Make personalised birth-

the card that shows through the shape you have cut out.

All in all, just let your imagination take over, and see what really original cards you can make.

CALENDARS

For those at Christmas to whom you like to give more

than a card, but not a proper present, why not make a calendar? Useful throughout the year, they can be as easy to make as you like. Follow these simple instructions, and you'll see how.

The simplest way of all is to find a pretty picture in an old magazine (or draw one on a piece of paper), cut it out and glue it on to a piece of cardboard. Make a hole in the top and knot through a piece of ribbon to hang it up by. Rule up twelve pieces of paper with seven squares across and seven down. Leave a blank space at the top in which you can write the name of each month. Then fill in the days of the week along the top row of boxes starting with Sunday. With a 'next year's' diary or calendar to follow, write in the dates of each month on the correct days. Make two holes at the top of the sheets, above the name of the month, and two holes to correspond on the cardboard beneath the picture. Thread a length of ribbon through so the month sheets are attached to the cardboard, and tie it at the back. Then each month can be torn off as it goes by.

Day-by-day calendar

You will need twelve long rectangular pieces of paper.

Glue or paint a picture on the top half of each. (You could use old Christmas cards or postcards cut to size.) Then rule up the bottom part of the pages as shown on previous page, writing in the days and dates for each month and leaving a space for engagements to be written in later. Write the S for Sunday in a different colour each time, so it can be seen at a glance where each week begins.

Mrs. Mop calendar
Draw and cut out a 'Mrs. Mop' shape as shown on previous page. Attach a little piece of ribbon to the back of her hat for hanging. Rule and write out monthly sheets like the ones needed for the simple calendar and staple them in position to make Mrs. Mop's apron.

PRESENTS FOR THE FAMILY & FRIENDS

Try to make presents for your family and friends at birthdays and Christmas. It will save your hard-saved or earned pocket money, and they will value them much more for the thought and care you have put into them.

Here are some ideas.

For Mother
Dressing table tidies
You will need:
For the tissue holder:
Patterned cotton fabric
1 metre lace or daisy trimming
2 small safety pins
Thin ribbon
Needle, Thread, Scissors
Box of tissues
For the cotton wool bag:
Cotton fabric approx. 20×34 cm
$\frac{1}{2}$ metre of cording
Embroidery thread
Needle, Sewing thread, Scissors
Coloured cotton wool balls
What to do:
To make the tissue holder measure the length, height and width of the box of tis-

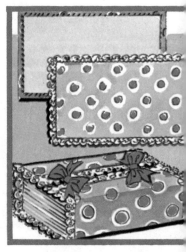

sues. Add together height and width measurements and double the result. Cut the fabric so it measures 4 cm **more** than this measurement one way and 4 cm more than the length of the box the other (i.e. if the box is 25 cm long×7 cm high×11 cm wide your fabric should be 40×29 cm).

Turn in and stitch a hem all the way round the piece of fabric (see page 45). Sew the lace trimming round the edge on the opposite side to the hem, using small hemming stitches or back stitch (see page 45), whichever is most suitable to the trimming you have. Carefully take the tissues from the box so they are still in one block. Wrap the trimmed fabric round them (trimmed side outside) and attach the

two sides together about 4 cm from either end with the safety pins. Tie little bows on to the top of the pins to hide them and pull the top tissue through the hole.

To make the cotton-wool tidy fold the material so it measures 20×17 cm and back stitch along the long edge (opposite the fold) and along one shorter edge to make a bag. Turn a hem to the wrong side at the open end of the bag and stitch round leaving a 2-cm gap unstitched. Turn the bag the right way out. Slip a safety pin through one end of the cording and thread it round the hem. Undo the safety pin and knot ends of the cord.

On one side of the bag write the words COTTON WOOL in pencil, then embroider the letters in chain or stem stitch (see page 47). Fill the bag with the cotton wool balls.

For Father
A folder for private papers
Make this folder for your father, and he'll have no excuse to lose his private papers again!

You will need:
4 pieces of cardboard 32×23 cm
2 pieces of wallpaper 36×27 cm
1 piece of wallpaper 10×27 cm

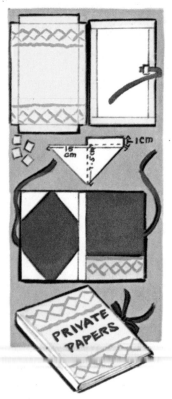

Cartridge paper
Ribbon 40 cm long
Felt-tip pens, Paint
Glue, Sticky tape

What to do:

Paint one side of two pieces of cardboard. Smear glue round the edges of the two remaining pieces and press down onto the larger pieces of wallpaper. Cut out a small square of wallpaper at each corner as shown. Smear glue along the cardboard, fold the wallpaper over and press down.

Cut the ribbon in half. Place one length in the middle of one long side on the wrong side of each wallpapered piece of cardboard and hold in place with sticky tape. Tape the other bit of ribbon to the equivalent opposite side, on the wrong side of the remaining wallpapered card.

Place the smaller piece of wallpaper across one end of one painted piece of card, overlapping 2 cm at either side and the bottom (to make a pocket). Fold the surplus to the back, cut corners as before and glue to secure. Then glue the two painted pieces of card to the wrong side of the wallpapered card. (N.B. The piece with the pocket should be on top of the piece of card with the ribbon on the right-hand side.)

Cut two pieces of cartridge paper 8 cm wide and the same length as the pieces of cardboard (top to bottom). Fold lengthways and open out. Place the two sides of the folder on top of each other (painted sides inside and tapes at the right) and glue one piece of cartridge paper along the left-hand edge to form a spine. Glue the other piece on the inside to reinforce it.

Cut four triangular pieces of cartridge paper with an

extra tab as shown. Fold along the dotted line and glue the tab over the edge. Cut off the surplus. Smear glue on the outside corners of the folder, push the cartridge paper corner pieces on and press down.

Tie the tapes at the side in a neat bow and write MY PRIVATE PAPERS on the front of the folder with felt-tip pens.

For Brother
Desk set
Make this smart desk set for your brother—it will encourage him to keep all his pens and pencils in one place!

You will need:
Thick cardboard approx. 22×10 cm
Thick cardboard approx. 8×12 cm
Cardboard tube approx. 16 cm long and 5 cm in diameter
Roll of sticky paper
Paints, Varnish
Felt-tip pens
Glue

What to do:
Cut the tube in half and glue each piece to the larger piece of cardboard approximately 1 cm from either end. Press down firmly to make sure they have stuck. Cut the other piece of cardboard into four strips, each 8×3 cm, and glue one long edge of these in between the tubes to form a square. Reinforce the tubes and square by sticking short lengths of sticky paper on the inside of them and to the base. Paint the desk set all over with a bright colour. Then, with a black felt-tip pen, write the words PENS on one tube, PENCILS on the other and ODDS & ENDS on one side of the square. Complete by varnishing with two or three coats of clear varnish.

For Sister
A string of beads
You will need:
Orange and grapefruit

peel
Sticky tape
Sharp knife
Thin knitting needles
Strong thread, Scissors

What to do:

Cut the orange and grapefruit peel into strips about 1 cm wide and 4 cm long. Wind these round the knitting needles and stick the ends with sticky tape to hold them in place. Put them in the airing cupboard for several days to dry (the peel will become hard and dark). When it is quite dry, remove the Sellotape and thread the 'beads' onto strong thread. Knot the ends.

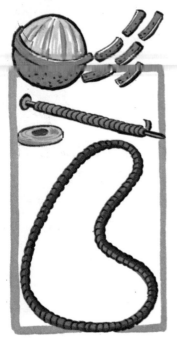

For Grandma and Grandpa

A bookmark each

For Grandma's:

You will need:
Strip of felt approx. 4×15 cm
Contrasting colour embroidery threads
Needle, Scissors

For Grandpa's:

You will need:
Thin card, approx. 5×15 cm
Felt-tip pens
Scissors

What to do:

To make Grandma's bookmark, work a border of blanket stitch all round the felt (see page 46). Plan out the word BOOKMARK to read down the marker in pencil. Embroider it in chain or stem stitch.

To make Grandpa's

bookmark, draw a picture of his face at the top of the card strip. Colour it in with felt-tip pens and cut round it so you have a long strip of card with a portrait of Grandpa at the top! Cut the bottom 4 or 5 cm into a point. Colour in a border round the edge with felt-tip pens and write something suitable like 'I have read to here' or 'This marks my place' on the marker.

For Your Friend

A set of matchbox doll's house furniture

You will need:
Matchboxes (see individual items for how many)
Oddments of felt, fabric and paper
Spent matchsticks
Glue, Scissors, Paints
Cotton wool

What to do:

Armchair: Glue two matchboxes to the sides of one flat one and glue an upright one at the back as shown opposite. Paint or glue fabric all over.

Settee: Glue two matchboxes side by side with one at either end as shown. Glue two upright matchboxes at the back. Paint or glue fabric all over.

Cushions: Make tiny cushions by cutting small squares of fabric, placing the wrong sides together and stitching round three sides. Turn to the right side, stuff with a tiny piece of cotton wool and oversew the fourth edge.

Card table: Squash the outer part of a matchbox flat. Make sure it stays flat by putting tiny spots of glue on the inside and putting it under a heavy book till the glue dries. Cut a piece of green felt the same size and glue it to one side. Glue four spent matchsticks to the underneath part to make table legs.

Television: Paint a matchbox light brown all over. Cut out a square of grey paper and glue it in place for the screen. Paint on tiny black dots for the knobs.

For Baby

A pompom rabbit

You will need:

Thin card

Ball of pink wool and oddments of white wool

Pink and black felt

Blue ribbon

Needle, Scissors

What to do:

Make two pink pompoms (see pages 37-8) from cardboard rings 6 cm and 4 cm in diameter. Sew the smaller one on top of the larger one to make the rabbit's head. Cut two long ears in pink felt and two little eyes in black felt and sew to the rabbit's head.

Wind three tiny tight balls of white wool and sew two to the front for little paws and one to the back for a tail. Tie a bow of blue ribbon round the rabbit's neck. Make a loop from another length of ribbon and sew it into the top of his head so the toy can hang up on the pram or baby's cot.

For Anyone

A collage picture

Collage is a really fun thing to do! It means making a picture or a design out of bits of fabric or trimmings, or buttons, or bottle tops, or string, or anything at all! Here are two collages for you to try: one is a conventional picture and the other is a real abstract.

In general, decide on the person to whom you are going to give your collage before you begin to make it, so you can choose a suitable subject to depict.

Fabric collage

Turning an already drawn picture into a collage will help you to get the feel of the art generally. You could use any picture, one on a greetings card, one cut from a magazine or one you have drawn. Choose one which has clear and definite outlines. We will give specific instructions for doing ours

here, but they will apply in principle to any picture you choose.

You will need:
Fairly large picture
Strong cardboard
Oddments of fabric
Oddments of wool or embroidery thread
Narrow velvet ribbon or trimming
Glue
Tracing paper, Pencil
Scissors

What to do:
Make a tracing of the main outlines of the picture—in this case it would be the boy's body, the girl's shoulders, and the main outline of the car and wheels. (Don't worry about the faces, you can leave them as they are in the picture.) Cut the tracing into pieces so you can use them as paper patterns to cut out the fabric. Cut out the boy's body to his waist, his trousers and shoes, the girl's shoulders, the car body, wheels, window and door in suitable fabrics. Cut out the boy's arms and hands in pink felt.

Glue the picture onto a piece of cardboard. Place all the fabric pieces on to the corresponding parts of the picture and glue them down, using glue very sparingly. Cut short lengths of wool—or better still stranded embroidery thread— and glue it in place to make the children's hair.

Glue the velvet ribbon or trimming round the picture to frame it.

Abstract collage

You will need:

Thick cardboard (any size you like!)

All or any of the following:

    small stones or pebbles
    a few screws and nails
    bottle tops
    buttons
    beads
    bits of string
    paper clips
    (and anything else you can think of!)

All-purpose glue

White spray paint

What to do:

Cut off a 3-cm strip from each edge of the cardboard and glue it back at right angles to make a 'frame'. Arrange all the bits and pieces you have on to the card in an abstract design. (Coil the bits of string into interesting shapes.) Rearrange everything until you have a design that pleases you, then, using the glue sparingly, stick each piece to the card. When the glue has dried, spray the whole creation, frame and all, white. Looks dramatic, doesn't it?

PRETTY PARCELS

Now for some original ideas for wrapping up your parcels!

Newspaper parcel

A smart idea for father's present—and economical too! Take the front page of his favourite newspaper and wrap his present in it so the headlines are displayed. Tie a brightly coloured ribbon round it and there you are! Write your message to him across the paper in large, bold letters using a thick felt-tip pen.

Crackerjack

Roll some plain coloured shiny paper into a tube about 25 cm long and glue the edge to hold it in place. Twist the paper about 6 cm from one end to make a cracker end and tie it with cotton thread. Slip the present into the open end (sister's necklace, for example) and then twist the other end

in the same way. Decorate a sticky label with felt-tip pens, write the message on it and stick it to the middle of the cracker.

Dice cube
This is a good way to wrap a square box. Wrap it neatly with a plain coloured paper (white is best), then glue coloured circles on each side to represent the numbers on a dice (one to six).

You could make a domino parcel in a similar way, if you were wrapping a flattish box. Use black wrapping or tissue paper. Tie a narrow white ribbon round the middle and glue on white circles of paper to look like domino spots.

Clock face
Round boxes can be made into clock faces—fun for young members of the family. Cut a circle of plain paper the same size as the box and glue it to the lid. Write in the numbers 1-12 round the circle like a clock face. Cut out a large hand and a small hand from thin card. Colour them and glue them into the middle to read whatever time you like.

FESTIVE FOOD
The different festivities of the year give you a special and fun way to help your mother in the kitchen by preparing some festive food. Remember the rules for working in the kitchen: Don't begin anything without asking your mother first. Make sure she is there to help you when handling sharp knives and hot pans or when lighting the oven. Wash your hands and put on an apron before you begin. Collect everything you need at the start of a recipe and always make sure you wash up everything and leave the kitchen spotless.

Christmas Fare
Mince pies
  You will need:
  Ingredients:
  4 oz (113 grammes) plain flour
  2 oz (57 grammes) mar-

garine
Pinch of salt
2 tblspns cold water (approx.)
4 oz (113 grammes) mincemeat (approx.)
Icing sugar
Utensils:
Sieve
Bowl
Tablespoon
Teaspoon
Knife
Rolling pin
Pastry cutters
Patty tin
Skewer

What to do:

First you make the pastry. This is a basic method and can be used for making all sorts of pies and tarts. The secret of good pastry-making is to keep everything as cold as possible while making—use cold water and handle the dough as little and quickly as possible— then cook it in a very hot oven. A useful saying to remember is 'Cold while making—hot while baking'.

1. Sieve the flour and salt into a clean bowl.

2. Cut up the margarine into little cubes and put it in the bowl with the flour. With your fingertips rub the fat and the flour together until the mixture looks like bread-crumbs and all the lumps have gone.

3. Add the water and mix to a firm dough, using a round-bladed knife.

4. Turn out on to a floured surface and roll out until it is about 0.5 cm thick.

5. Cut into an equal number of large and slightly smaller rounds, using pastry cutters. Place the large rounds in the patty tin.

6. Spoon a teaspoon or so of mincemeat on each.

7. Dampen the edges of the pastry with a little water and press the smaller rounds on top. Press the edges together gently to seal them.

8. Make a hole in the middle of each with a skewer. Ask your mother to bake the pies for you at regulo 6 or 400°F for 20 to 30 minutes.

9. Put on a wire tray to cool and sprinkle with sieved icing sugar.

Christmas cake

You will need:

Ingredients:

8 oz (226 grammes) self-raising flour

4 oz (113 grammes) butter

4 oz (113 grammes) soft brown sugar

$\frac{1}{2}$ teaspoon mixed spice

2 oz (57 grammes) raisins

2 oz (57 grammes) currants

1 oz (28 grammes) glacé cherries

2 oz (57 grammes) mixed cut peel

3 eggs

Little milk if necessary

Utensils:

Round deep cake tin

Greaseproof paper

Bowls

Wooden spoon

Metal spoon

Fork

Sieve

Knife

Wire tray

What to do:

1. Grease the tin. Cut a circle of greaseproof paper the same size as the tin and put it in the bottom. Line round the sides with a strip of greaseproof paper and grease on the inside again.

2. Cut the glacé cherries in half. Mix them with the currants, raisins and cut peel. Add the mixed spice and a teaspoon of flour.

3. Beat the butter and sugar together thoroughly with a wooden spoon until the mixture is creamy.

4. Break one egg into a small bowl and beat it with a fork. Add little by little to the butter and sugar mixture, beating all the time. Repeat with the other two eggs.

5. Sieve half the flour into the bowl and fold it into the mixture with half the fruit mixture, using a metal spoon. Repeat with the remainder of the flour and fruit. The mixture should drop easily from the spoon. If it doesn't, mix in a little milk.

6. Spoon the mixture into the prepared cake tin and ask your mother to bake it for you at regulo 3, 325°F, for about one and a half hours. (It should be firm to the touch.)

7. Leave to cool in the tin for

a little while, then turn it on to a wire tray.

To ice the cake

You will need:

Ingredients:

1 lb (456 grammes) icing sugar

2 egg whites

Few drops lemon juice

1 tblspn apricot jam

Utensils:

Sieve

Pastry brush

Bowls

Wooden spoon

Metal spoon

Knife

Fork

What to do:

(Keep the egg yolks and make scrambled egg from them for breakfast.)

1. If the cake isn't quite flat, cut off the very top to make it do.

2. Rub the apricot jam through a sieve and brush it over the top and sides of the cake.

3. Lightly whisk the egg whites with a fork so they are frothy but not stiff.

4. Sieve in the icing sugar, about one-quarter at a time, and beat it in thoroughly between sievings. Beat in the lemon juice.

5. Put a large spoonful of icing on the top, and spread it over the top with a knife.

6. Spread the remainder of the icing round the sides. Then, with the knife, 'lift' the icing up into peaks all over, so it looks like ruffled snow.

7. Decorate with holly leaves, model Father Christmases, reindeer, or what you will!

Meringue snowmen

Another tea-time treat.

You will need:

1 egg white

2 oz (57 grammes) caster sugar

½ oz (14 grammes) icing sugar

½ teaspoon cocoa

Utensils:

Whisk

Bowl

Metal spoon

Flat baking tray

Greaseproof paper

2 teaspoons

What to do:

1. Put a sheet of greaseproof paper on the tray.

2. Whisk egg white until it is

very stiff.

3. Whisk in half the sugar, a teaspoonful at a time. Fold the rest in quickly with a wooden spoon.

4. Spoon 10-12 blobs on the baking tray, and top with small blobs to make heads.

5. Ask your mother to bake them in the lowest part of the oven at regulo ¾, 225°F, for about two hours.

6. Cool on a wire tray. When they are quite cold, mix the icing sugar and cocoa together and stir in just enough water to make a very thick cream. Dip a skewer into this icing and use it to give each snowman eyes and a mouth.

Christmas sweets

Make these to add to the Christmas fare or as a present for someone.

Chocolate truffles

You will need:
Ingredients:
4 oz (113 grammes) icing sugar
3 oz (85 grammes) cocoa powder
3 tblspns double cream
1 teaspoonful of rum
Chocolate vermicelli
Utensils:
Sieve
Bowl
Wooden spoon
Paper sweet cases

What to do:

1. Sieve the icing sugar and the cocoa into a bowl.

2. Add the cream and rum and mix together well.

3. Dust your hands with icing sugar and then roll the mixture into small even-sized balls with your hands.

4. Roll each ball in chocolate vermicelli and put them in the paper sweet cases.

Birthday time

The only food that could be called 'traditional' at birthdays is a birthday cake—and that can vary tremendously, both in flavouring and in the shape you can make. On the next page you see how to make a train from a swiss roll, but there are all sorts of ways you could decorate an ordinary round sponge cake to make it a special birthday treat. You will find some ideas on pages 114-18 for

food to make for a birthday party.

Birthday express

You will need:

Ingredients:

3 eggs

$3\frac{1}{2}$ oz (100 grammes) caster sugar

$\frac{1}{2}$ oz (14 grammes) cocoa

$2\frac{3}{4}$ oz (78 grammes) flour

1 tablespoon very hot water

Utensils:

Saucepan of hot water

Bowl

Whisk

Sieve

Metal spoon

Swiss roll tin

What to do:

1. Line the swiss roll tin with a sheet of non-stick cooking paper.

2. Break the eggs into a bowl and add the sugar.

3. Stand the bowl over a saucepan of hot water and whisk mixture until it turns thick, pale and frothy.

4. Remove bowl from the saucepan and continue whisking until the mixture has cooled.

5. Sieve the flour and cocoa into the mixture together and fold in, using a metal spoon. When you have nearly finished doing this, add the tablespoon of very hot water and fold that in too.

6. Pour the mixture into the tin and ask your mother to bake it for you for about 7-10 minutes at regulo 6, 400°F.

7. When the cake is cooked, turn it out immediately onto a sheet of greaseproof paper laid on top of a damp cloth. Roll it up, using the paper to help. Leave to cool.

To decorate the cake:

You will need:

Ingredients:

8 oz (226 grammes) icing sugar

4 oz (113 grammes) butter

6 level tblspns cocoa

Vanilla essence

Boiling water

4 round chocolate biscuits

Chocolate buttons

Marshmallows

Utensils:

Bowl

Sieve

74

Wooden spoon
Knife

What to do:

1. Soften the butter, sieve in icing sugar and beat together.

2. Add cocoa dissolved in a little boiling water and a few drops of vanilla essence. Beat together well.

3. Unroll the swiss roll and spread the inside thinly with butter icing.

4. Roll up again and spread the remainder of the icing over the outside. Smooth with a knife and stand cake on a plate.

5. Put the chocolate biscuits at the side to look like wheels. Make some 'buffers' and a chimney with marshmallows. Put a row of chocolate buttons along side of cake as decoration.

Peppermint creams

You will need:

Ingredients:

1 lb (456 grammes) icing sugar

1 egg white

1 teaspoon lemon juice

4 drops of peppermint essence

2 oz (57 gms) chocolate

Utensils:

Sieve, Bowls
Wooden spoon
Small pastry cutter
Skewer
Saucepan of hot water
Teaspoon

What to do

1. Sieve the icing sugar into a bowl.

2. Add the lemon juice and egg white and mix it all together.

3. Put 4 drops of peppermint essence into the mixture, using a skewer dipped into the essence bottle. Stir well into the mixture.

4. Sprinkle surface of working area with icing sugar. Turn the mixture on to it and knead it with your hands.

5. Flatten it out with your fingers and stamp out tiny rounds with the pastry cutter. Roll up the left-over bits, press them out and stamp out some more.

6. Give some of the peppermint creams a chocolate top. Break up the chocolate and put the pieces in a bowl. Put the bowl in a saucepan of very hot water so the

chocolate melts.

7. When the peppermint creams are quite crisp (they will take about half an hour), put a little blob of melted chocolate on top. Very quickly rub this round the top with the bowl of the teaspoon to coat the top evenly.

8. Leave to harden.

Easter eggs

Decorating eggs at Easter time is a tradition that goes back for generations. Get up early on Easter day and make some 'egg' surprises for your family.

First you must hard boil the eggs. To do this, put them in a saucepan of cold water, put it over the heat and bring the water to the boil. Allow it to boil for at least five minutes, so the eggs are really hard, and then remove them from the pan and put them straight into cold water. When they have cooled down, you can take them out and paint funny faces on them with felt-tip pens. Make up little hats out of oddments of fabric or knitting beforehand and use these to top the eggs.

Alternatively you could make faces, or just pretty patterns, by sticking on seeds, apple pips, lentils and so on. Fix them on with tiny spots of clear household glue and put them in position with a pair of tweezers.

Eggs dyed all over in plain bright colours look lovely too. You can dye them any colour you like by using a commercial cold dye. Mix it up as directed on the packet (don't forget to wear rubber gloves) and immerse the hard-boiled eggs for at least thirty minutes, stirring occasionally with a wooden spoon (one kept specially for dyeing!). Remove the eggs with a draining spoon and leave them to dry. If you want to give them a glossy shine, you could rub them over with a little salad oil.

Another way to dye eggs, and this is more fun in a way, is to use natural materials. You can use onion skins for a lovely russet colour, tea leaves for a goldy brown, spinach for green, and red cabbage for a red colour. Put a handful of whichever of these you like, with the eggs, into individual saucepans and hard boil the eggs for thirty minutes or so to give a deep colour.

Line a wicker basket with some straw and pop in a selection of your dyed or decorated eggs to make a lovely centrepiece for your Easter breakfast table.

Things to Make and Do

ENTERTAINMENT FOR ALL

Putting on a play, either one you act yourself with your friends, or a puppet show, is a great way of entertaining people. It would give tremendous pleasure to elderly people, for example, who may not be able to get out and about very much. Plan the play and rehearse it well beforehand so you are fairly professional when the big day comes. If you have to learn words, make sure you do so thoroughly so there

are no awkward pauses during the performance. If it is a mime, make sure all your actions are so well rehearsed that they are almost second nature. Make all your costumes and any props you may need well before the show so you have lots of time to try them on and make necessary alterations. (There are some costume and prop ideas on the following pages.)

Remember that, besides the actors, you will need a prompter (in the 'wings' of your stage with a copy of the play just in case anyone forgets their words); some extra helpers to assist with costume and scenery

changing if necessary; an announcer for the play; and maybe someone to work the curtains if you have been able to fix some at the front of the stage. Remember, too, that all these people are just as important to the success of the play as the actors on the stage.

In all acting, remember that you must speak your words very clearly and rather more slowly than you would normally. Face the audience as much of the time as possible, and if you are miming you must make your actions very clear and definite, exaggerating them somewhat, so the audience can see immediately just what you are trying to portray.

Don't 'mask' other actors by standing in front of them, and give your part only what it demands—no points are scored for 'over acting'! So don't shout louder than is necessary and don't swagger around trying to steal the limelight. You won't, in fact—you'll just look silly!

The play
Count up the number of people among you and your friends who are going to take part and choose the play accordingly. Don't

choose a play with a cast of twenty-five, if only three or four of you want to be involved, but on the other hand if there are lots of you don't choose a play which only has a couple of parts!

Best of all would be to write your own play together with your friends. If you do this, remember that you probably won't want to make it much longer than an hour (with an interval in the middle). Plan the plot before you start to write. Points to remember are:

1. Make the story exciting and dramatic so that it will hold the audience's attention more than one in which nothing very much happens.
2. Introduce the main characters quite quickly at the beginning so that the audience knows at once who everybody is and how they are related or connected with each other.
3. Give your play a 'beginning', a 'middle' and an 'end'. In other words, let the audience know as soon as possible what the plot is. Then build up the action to a dramatic point by the interval. Develop the theme a little more in the second half, and then bring the play to a climax by solving the problem,

killing the villain or whatever! Once you have reached this point, you should end the play quite quickly.

To start you off, here are some title and plot suggestions for plays you could make up and act with your friends.

1. A day at the seaside with your family and some friends. Perhaps one of your friends gets marooned on the rocks and you have to get the coastguard to help, and all the time the tide is coming in . . .

2. You and some friends go off to explore a deserted house in the middle of some dark woods. Perhaps the house isn't as deserted as you thought . . .
3. You could base a play on a well-known folk or fairy tale, such as Little Red Riding Hood, Cinderella or Snow White and the Seven Dwarfs.

Costumes

Making costumes is all part of the fun of putting on a play. Nothing need be expensive—in fact you should be able to find all your 'costume materials' around the house.

Keep a dressing-up box for old clothes from grown-ups and improvise as many costumes from this as possible. Collect old hats and boots and shoes. Boots and shoes can be painted in bright colours (provided they really are old and not wanted any more), and hats can be transformed by tying

scarves, ribbons or bands of crêpe paper round them, or pushing long feathers into them. Wigs, costume jewellery, sun-glasses and old spectacles, scarves, belts and gloves will all come in handy. Remember cotton wool is good for beards, and

you can make thin people into very fat people by tying cushions round their middles and then putting large clothes on them.

Large paper sacks are super for dressing up. Cut

out holes for head and arms, then paint the sack to be a soldier's or sailor's or policeman's uniform, or a playing card (especially good for Alice in Wonderland), or a robot or just about anything. Add decorations by gluing on strips of paper, washed milk bottle tops for silver buttons, foil or crêpe paper scales to be a bird or a dragon.

Old sheets are invaluable for costumes, too. They can be dyed any colour (black for a wizard or witch's cloak, for example), or, left white, they make good 'ghostie garb' just draped over you. Cut out a hole for your head, tie them round your shoulders and waist with gold ribbon and you have a Grecian costume. Use sheets for Roman and Arabian costumes as well as brides and princesses.

Coloured tights with polo-neck jumpers the same colour are good dressing-up standbys. Worn together with a tail made from an old stocking and sewn on, you can turn yourself into cats, mice, lions—almost any kind of animal—just by adding a simple mask. An old pair of gloves with glued-on cardboard claws complete the disguise! They are good, too, as the 'groundwork' of other costumes. Add a jacket, some boots, a hat with a feather, a cloak and a few paper frills here and there, and you are a dashing musketeer!

Crêpe paper is very useful when making costumes. Taped onto elastic or a length of ribbon and cut into strips, it makes good grass skirts. It is also very good for making ruffles and frills.

To make a cuff frill: Fold two lengths of crêpe paper con-

certina fashion. Cut off one end at a slant to make points. Open out the paper and sew, tape or staple it to the cuff edge of a blouse, dress or jacket.

To make a collar frill: Cut a large circle of crêpe paper,

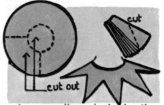

cut a smaller circle in the middle for the neck and cut out one-quarter of the whole circle. Fold the remainder into a concertina fan, and at the wider end cut off the corner to make points. Open out and sew, tape or staple it to the neck edge of the garment.

To make a cloak: Fold over the top of a long strip of

crêpe paper to a depth of about 16 cm. Make two lines of stitching, about 8-12 cm from the folded edge, and thread a length of tape through. Pull up, to gather the crêpe paper, and tie the tapes round your neck.

Masks and Hats

Really use your imagination when devising masks, and you should come up with some highly original ideas. Here are some suggestions to start you off.

Probably the easiest masks of all to make are face masks from thin card (cereal packets are ideal). The easiest way is to cut the card into a circular shape

fringe of glued-on lengths of wool.

Paper bags make good masks, too. You can use large ones, with eye and nose holes cut out and pulled right over your head, decorated to represent whatever you like; or you can use smaller ones just pulled over the top of your head. Again they are good for animal heads—stick on

(or even leave it oblong for a strangely shaped face!), cut out eye holes and paint on the features of the particular mask you want. Make small holes in the side and thread a length of elastic through so you can just slip the mask on over your head.

To make this kind of mask a bit more elaborate, add ears, cut out and stuck on, or cut at the same time as you make the mask; stick on bits of coloured paper for cheek spots or round the eyes to give exotic eye 'make-up'. Top it with a

ears of various shapes and whiskers and paint on the features.

Make a bird mask by gluing on a thin, orange card beak to the front of a paper bag, cutting out eye holes and decorating the rest of it with paper 'feathers'.

Hats and helmets are easily made from cardboard. A strip of cardboard twisted into a tube and stuck or stapled down forms the basis of a soldier's helmet. Paint it silver or red and add a little peak to it. Or cut out eye holes and pull it right

over your head for a crusader type helmet—or a spaceman's headgear.

Make a pirate's tricorn from a large circle of black paper, about 50 cm in diameter. Cut out a 25-cm diameter circle in the middle, then cut once through the remaining ring. Overlap the cut ends, until the circle

'stands up', glue the ends and staple the front of the hat in a wedge shape. Paint a skull and crossbones on the side. Spotted handkerchiefs or cotton squares make good pirate gear, too, and black eye patches complete the ensemble. Make them from small oval shapes of black paper, threaded on to a length of tape which you can tie round your head.

Wizards' hats can be made by twisting a semicircle of black card into a cone and gluing the sides together. Witches' hats can be made like that, too, but need to have a circular brim added. Or you can be very clever and make a witch's mask and hat all in one go. Cut a large semi-circle of white card and twist it into a cone. Stick down the sides. Slip it down over your face and get someone to mark where your eyes and nose will come. Cut out holes in these places and then draw a nasty witchy face round them (a grinning mouth with a few ugly teeth drawn in will look good and witchy!). Cut a circle of card and cut a smaller circle inside it. Slip this over the top of the cone to make the brim of the hat. Paint the brim and the part above it black.

Make Indian headdresses by cutting out large

thin card 'feathers' and painting them bright colours. Then stitch, tape or staple them to a length of coloured braid. Drape a patterned blanket round your shoulders and you'll make a splendid Indian chief!

Make crowns for kings and queens and fairy princesses from strips of paper painted gold, cut into points along one long edge and glued or stapled to make a circle that fits your head. Decorate with washed bottle-top 'jewels'.

Props
Acting props fall into two categories—those you want to supplement your costume and those you need to create the right surroundings on the stage.

Costume props are such things as swords and spears, magic wands, shields, bows and arrows, fairy wings, maybe, and jewellery, too, if you haven't got sufficient of the costume type in your dressing-up box.

Cardboard is the obvious material for swords, cutlasses and daggers. Cut out a suitably sized and shaped 'blade' and paint it silver. Glue a short strip across it at right angles for the handle, or else make slots in either end of the strip and slide it on to the blade (best for sword handles).

Cut out circular or oblong shields. Paint them silver or black or any colour and glue on cardboard or 'stick' handles at the back to carry them.

Cardboard boxes make good spacemen or dalek gear. Strap small ones to your back for air-packs or decorate larger ones with knobs and dials to represent a dalek. (Cut out head and armholes and slip it on yourself.)

Make big pendants and earrings from circles of cardboard, painted or decorated with buttons and sequins and hung from lengths of card. Cardboard is good for wide bangles, too, and curtain rings also make good pirate or gypsy earrings.

Magic and fairy wands are easy to make by gluing a cardboard star—painted gold or silver—to a length of thin dowelling. Make fairy wings by twisting wire into circles or oval shapes and gluing or taping coloured tissue paper over them. Tie some tapes to the middle to tie them on, or sew them onto your costume.

Stage Props

Stage props and scenery can be as simple or complicated as you like and you can rely on your audience to use their imagination!

Strong cardboard boxes draped with a sheet dyed green make a good 'mossy bank', but don't leap on to it too enthusiastically, in case you go right through! Make trees, if you really need them, by cutting simple tree shapes from thick cardboard and painting them. You will have to prop them up from behind.

If you need a scenic background, you could paint a landscape on large sheets of paper stuck together and

suspended from a pole se-
cured high up on the wall. It
is probable, however, that
your play will look just as
effective played against a
plain backdrop of a dyed
sheet suspended from
poles.

If your story is a tale of
the Wild West, you can make
good Indian wigwams by
draping a blanket round

three poles tied together
near to the top. (This is also
a good way of making a
fortune-telling tent, too, and
empty goldfish bowls turned
upside down make super
crystal balls!) You could

have fun making a totem pole, which would make your Wild West stage seem very real. Paint wild and colourful faces on several cardboard boxes of the same size and then glue them one on top of another.

If you are enacting a pirate story make a 'ship' out of chairs and table put on their sides on the floor but arranged in such a way that you don't continually fall over them! Even if it doesn't look quite like a ship, you will soon have the audience thinking of it as one if your acting is good.

Make a skull and cross-bones flag and a large ship's wheel. To do this, cut a circle of cardboard and stick cardboard spokes across it so they protrude 10 cm or so beyond the edge. Tape it to a chair. Make a telescope from a cardboard tube painted silver and remember to hold it up to the eye that is not covered by a black patch! A few bloodcurdling noises, and you'll have your audience quaking in their seats!

MAKING MUSIC

Sometimes it is fun to have a little musical accompani-ment to your play. You could use a record player, but that is really cheating. If there is a piano in the room, a talented person amongst you could play it, or better still you could make some instruments of your own.

Simple Chimes

Make these simple chimes by suspending ten empty milk bottles from strong string tied to a pole (such as a broom handle). Hang this between two chairs and secure it in place by tying it. (The milk bottles must be off the ground.) Fill the milk bottles with varying amounts of water and then

tap them with wooden sticks. You will get a different sound from each, so experiment to make tunes, noises like bells ringing and so on.

Maracas

Maracas originated in Latin America. In their original form they were gourds filled with small pebbles and seeds and used as a percussion instrument. Usually played in pairs, they make a lovely gentle, swishing, rattling noise.

Make them from old plastic bottles (the sort that hold washing-up liquid). Wash these out well and then coat the outside evenly with a few layers of papier mâché (see page 102). About half fill the bottles with dried seeds, rice or tiny pebbles and then push lengths of dowelling well down into the bottle neck. Wedge it with strips of newspaper if necessary and secure it with more strips of newspaper and glue. When the papier mâché is really dry, paint and varnish your maracas.

It is not absolutely necessary to cover the bottle with papier mâché, but it produces a gentler, more mellow sound. Now your maracas are ready. Play by holding them both in one

91

hand by the dowelling handles, and shaking them backwards and forwards rhythmically and evenly.

Drums

You can improvise an extremely crude drum by using an old biscuit tin and a couple of wooden spoons! It won't be very tonal, but it will probably bring your audience to attention quite quickly!

Make a slightly more sophisticated drum using an old, large paint tin. Remove both ends from it (use a tin opener on the fixed end). Then measure the diameter and draw two circles 8 cm larger on a piece of strong polythene sheeting. Cut these out. Paint the tin or decorate it with coloured paper cut-outs. Put a covering of glue all round the outside of the tin at one end, and stretch one circle of polythene over the end, pressing the edges down on to the glue, and keeping the whole thing as taut as possible. Secure in place by tying tightly with string, then repeat at the other end.

Use a couple of lengths of bamboo as drumsticks, or for a more subtle sound wrap and glue some lengths of foam rubber round one end of the bamboo sticks to make beaters.

PUPPETS

As we said at the beginning, you could also make your 'entertainment' a puppet

show—making your own puppets, of course.

Finger and hand puppets are the easiest to work, as well as to make. You could rig up a very simple 'stage' by suspending a curtain or a sheet on a pole hung between two chairs. Then you can kneel or crouch behind this, and work your puppets just above it.

Finger Puppets

Make a handful of 'woodland folk' finger puppets and make up a story about them. You could wear them all on one hand, or spread them over the fingers of both hands. Or make two of each of those listed below so you have one for every finger!

You will need:
Scraps of pink, golden brown, dark brown, grey and black felt
Paper

Felt-tip pens
Glue
Sewing cotton and needle

What to do:

Cut two ovals about 3 cm wide and 6 cm long in each of the coloured felts. Cut off the ends at one end to make flat edges. Oversew each pair of pieces together, leaving the flat edges open.

On the paper, draw with felt-tip pens a rabbit's face (with long ears and whiskers), a fox's face (shorter ears, a pointed nose and a sly smile), a mouse's face (large round ears and a timid expression), a badger's face (tiny ears and stripes of black and white) and a hedgehog's face (pointed nose and bristles on the top). Make each of these about 2 cm wide and 3 cm long—ears can protrude higher. Carefully cut out and glue each one to the felt bodies—the rabbit to the pink body, the fox to the

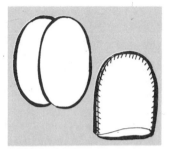

golden brown, the hedgehog to the darker brown, the badger to the black and the mouse to the grey. Slip them on to your fingers and you are ready to perform the story.

You could make it a story of what happens when the woodland folk meet some people. Make some little people puppets for your other hand. Make them in the same way, but instead of giving them paper faces, embroider the features, or glue on tiny felt eyes and mouths. Glue on bits of wool for hair.

They could act the Brownie Story.

Glove Puppets

There are masses of different ways to make glove puppets. Here are two ideas. You will need:

Paper and pencil
2 pieces of plain fabric, each about 20 cm square
Embroidery threads
Scraps of felt, fabric and wool
Sewing thread and needle

What to do:

Draw an outline shape like the one shown on to the paper and cut it out. Using

this as a paper pattern, cut out two shapes from the fabric squares. Place their right sides together and back-stitch round the edge (see page 45) leaving the bottom open. Turn to the right side and then work face and hair features to represent whatever puppet you are making.

For a girl: Cut out two eyes in felt and glue in place. Glue on two pink felt circles for cheeks and

embroider a mouth and eyebrows. Plait some long lengths of wool, tie the ends with bits of ribbon, and stitch the middle to the top of the puppet's 'head'. Make a frilly collar from a strip of fabric and stitch it round the puppet's 'neck'.

For a boy: Glue on felt face features and short bits of wool for hair. Give him an ordinary tie, or a bow tie made from a piece of fabric and glued in place.

Pull the puppets on to your hands, pushing your little fingers and thumbs into the side pieces to make 'arms'. Now they are ready to perform!

95

'Tube' Glove Puppets

You will need:

Scraps of fabric, felt and wool

Cardboard tube about 5 cm in diameter and 8 cm long

Felt-tip pens or paints

Sewing thread and needle

Glue

What to do:

Cut out the same puppet shape as before from two squares of fabric and sew round the edge. Turn to the right side. Paint a face on to the cardboard tube and glue on lengths of wool for hair.

Smear the inside of the tube (opposite end from hair) with glue and push the middle part of the fabric up into

it so the fabric sticks to the glue. Decorate the bottom part of the fabric in order to make the puppet's clothes.

PRINT-A-PATTERN

There are all sorts of ways you can print your own patterns, and once you've mastered a few techniques you can have lots of fun making your own personalised stationery, greetings cards and invitations, wrapping paper, pictures and posters, wall hangings and household items. If your parents agree, you might also print designs and motifs on some of your clothes, such as T-shirts and jeans.

Remember, printing can be a messy business, and so cover working area with lots of newspaper—if you want to be allowed to do it again! Wear old clothes or, better still, an old shirt or smock kept especially for the purpose, and keep lots of rags handy for wiping brushes, mopping up spills and so on.

Use the ideas on the following pages to spark off your imagination and see how many other ways you can devise to print interesting patterns.

Fruit and Vegetable Printing

Potato printing is an amusing and effective way of producing patterns. But you can use the same technique to print patterns with all sorts of vegetables. Here's what you do:

Cut a potato in half. Draw a shape on the flat surface and carve it out, using a table knife. The shape should be raised by about 1 cm.

Put some poster paint in a saucer. Dip the potato in, and then press it onto some paper—and you've made your first print!

Keep the shape you cut simple, with clearly defined lines. Try cutting the same shape out of both sides, but on one side make the design raised and on the other cut out the design itself, so the area around it is raised. For example, cut away the area around a triangle in one, and in the other the inside of the triangle, so you either print triangles or you print circles with white triangles in them.

Experiment with other vegetables and fruit. Many of them you just cut in half and use the flat surface for printing without even carving a design. Try it with apples and pears, mushrooms, radishes, cauliflower tops, carrots, celery stalks and so on. You can print beautiful flowers with an onion.

Look at the shapes—what objects do they suggest to you? (Cauliflower prints look like trees, radish prints could be a sun or a ball or a wheel.) Make a vegetable and fruit print picture, using all the natural shapes you can, and then carve potato prints for any other shapes you want.

Printing with leaves

Leaves make some of the most beautiful and delicate prints of all.

Here's what you do:

Collect a variety of leaves—those with fairly pronounced veins make the best prints. Cover the underside of the leaf with a layer of paint. Put it on a sheet of paper and cover it with another piece. Press down

97

on the top piece, then lift it and the leaf off.

Make small leaf prints at the top—or bottom—of writing paper, and on the back flap of an envelope. Or print random prints all over a sheet of paper in shades of red and gold and brown for autumn gift-wrap paper. Think of some more ideas.

Another way to make leaf prints is to lay them wrong side up on a sheet of newspaper. Cover them with the printing paper and then rub gently all over with a soft, or wax, crayon. The outline of the leaves will show delicately through your colouring and give you a lovely crayon print.

And one more idea—put a leaf, or leaves, on to a sheet of paper. Dip an old toothbrush into the paint and then spatter the paper with paint by brushing over the bristles with a finger. (Lots of newspaper for this one—paint spatters aren't always too easy to control!) Repeat with different colours and then lift up the leaf. You will have a lovely clear leaf print, surrounded by dense spots of colour.

Flower printing
You can make intricate prints with flowers, too. Here's what you do:
Collect simple, small flow-

ers—complete with their stalks and leaves if possible. Lay them on a sheet of paper and paint over their surfaces with a brush. Then quickly press the painted side of the flower on to another piece of paper. Lift it off and you are left with your print.

How about a very special calendar of flower prints, each month having a print of a flower that grows at that time of year? True, it would take about a year to complete your masterpiece, but it would really be something when it was finished! And in between times you can get on with some other, rather quicker, ideas.

Block Prints
You can make your own printing blocks, which you will be able to use over and over again.

Here's what you do:

Cut out a shape from very thick card and glue it to a block of wood. It could be an animal or a person or a flower or a geometric shape—or anything! Cover the shape with paint, press it on to the printing paper, and there you are. Experiment with different textures of cardboard, or cut up the shape and glue it with spaces in between so you have coloured and uncoloured areas mixed together.

Make a block alphabet by cutting out the letters from thick card and gluing them on to the wood. Remember to glue them back to front so they print the right way.

You can make printing blocks from Plasticine, too. Shape some Plasticine into a square or a round or an oblong. Press a pattern into the top, using a pen or the handle of a spoon or the blade of a screwdriver. Cover this surface with paint and press it onto a sheet of paper.

Blocks are good for printing posters or greetings cards or pictures.

Tie Dyeing

Now for some ways of printing cloth. Tie-dyeing is an ancient art which has become very popular. Besides all that newspaper and old clothes you have become used to in your printing sessions, you'll need some rubber gloves, too.

Here's what you do:

Take a square of white cotton. Find the centre and pick it up from this point. Smooth it into a long strip, still holding the centre point, and then either tie it at intervals with string or wind rubber bands around.

Make a dye bath of cold dye, following the instructions on the packet, and put in your tied-up strip. Leave it for the length of time the instructions tell you, then take it out, wash it and leave it to dry before undoing the ties. You will have a lovely sunburst pattern. If you like, you could leave the ties in place, add some more and dye it again, for a two-coloured sunburst.

If you are going to dye in two colours, remember you must dye the light colours first, and the effect you achieve will be to build up dark colours on the untied areas. Remember the basic colour-mix rules, too, so you can plan the colour result you want.

Red and yellow make orange
Yellow and blue make green
Blue and red make purple
Purple and orange make brown

For a different tie-dye effect, just crumple the cloth and tie string all over it. Dye it. Leave it to dry, tie some more and dye it again. You will have a lovely squiggly pattern.

Use the results of your tie-dyeing to make cushion covers, table napkins, head scarves—and what else?

Batik

Batik is another old craft that is enjoying modern popularity. It involves the use of hot wax—so be very careful.

Here's what you do:

Put some white household candles in a bowl. Place the bowl in a saucepan of hot water on the cooker. (Ask a grown-up for some help with this.) Put a piece of white cotton on some sheets of newspaper, and when the wax has melted, dribble it over the cloth in random lines and blodges, using an old teaspoon. Let it dry and harden. Mix up some cold dye as you did for the tie-dyeing and put the cloth in. Only the areas with no wax on them will be dyed.

Take it out of the dye. Let it dry and then put on some more wax in different places. Let it harden and

then crumple the cloth a bit so the wax cracks in places. This will give you lovely spidery lines of colour. Dye it again in another colour.

Let the cloth dry, then iron it between lots of sheets of brown paper with a hot iron to remove as much wax as possible.

Batik prints are good for dramatic wall hangings.

Painting on Fabric
Using specially prepared fabric dyes and a commercial 'fixer', you can paint directly on to fabric. Have a word with your mother before you cover all your clothes with painted designs, however!
Here's what you do:
Make up the dye, following the instructions on the packet. Put lots of newspaper around—if you are painting a pattern on the front of a T-shirt, put newspaper inside so the colour doesn't soak through to the back. Stuff jeans pockets with newspaper before painting pictures on them. Then map out a design on the surface and just paint it in.

You could cut out stencils from card, put them on the fabric and fill them in with paint. This will give you clear outlines. Cut out a stencil and use the cut-out frame on the front of a T-shirt. Then put the cut-out piece itself on the back and paint round it. Or you can use the blocks you made before, and coat them in fabric dyes rather than paint. Use your alphabet block to print your name on a T-shirt, or your Plasticine block to make patterns on jeans. You can print on fabric with vegetable cut-outs, too.

Alternatively you can just draw a pencil picture with very faint lines and just paint it as you would an ordinary picture.

Besides patterns on clothes, you could make borders on clothes or curtains, patterns or pictures on tea cosies—egg cosies, too—and many, many other things. Just use a little imagination.

MAKE-A-MODEL FARM
There are so many different ways to make models, so

many different materials you can use, and so many different ways of using them alone and together that it would fill several books to describe them all! On the following pages there are just a few ideas for you to begin with, but use them to help you think of others, too.

We have shown here how to combine all the ideas together to make a big model farm. You could make it on your own as a long project, or, to make it more fun, you could make it a venture with your friends. Each of the modelling ideas could be used on its own, of course, to make ornaments and presents.

Whether you are modelling on your own or with friends, remember to protect the area you are using from paint splashes, glue spills and the like with lots of old newspaper. Collect together everything you need for a project, and—most important of all—clear *everything* away when you have finished for the day, so no one can even see where you have been.

The Farm

You will need:

Thick card or hardboard, approx. 1 metre square
Old newspapers
Wallpaper paste
Cold water
Polystyrene food tray
Scissors, Paints, Paste brush

What to do:

Mix wallpaper paste with cold water (about $\frac{1}{2}$ litre of water to one dessertspoonful of paste gives the right consistency). Tear newspaper into long strips and brush each side with wallpaper paste. Press the strips down on to the board, covering it all over with about three layers of strips. At the bottom right-hand corner push the polystyrene food tray into the papier mâché and secure it with a few strips of pasted paper round the edge.

From about three-quarters of the way back on the board gradually build up more layers of paper strips to make a small 'hill' at the back of the board. Make it a gradual slope to a height of about 6 cm. Leave the board to dry.

Decide where you are going to put the house (when you have made it), then paint the area in front of it a browny colour for the yard. Paint the polystyrene food tray blue to make a pond, and then paint the rest of the board green, brown and gold for the fields.

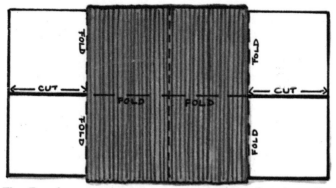

The Farmhouse

You will need:

Cardboard box, approx. 20×18×14 cm (18 cm is the measurement from top to bottom)

Thin card, approx. 40×20 cm and 4×16 cm

Thin string or raffia

Plasticine

Glue, Paints, Scissors

Sticky tape

What to do:

Cut the top and bottom off the box. Paint the outside white and mark the position of a front door in the middle of one long side. Mark windows on all walls; paint in these and the door. Cut along one side and the top of the door so it opens, and press on a tiny knob of Plasticine as a door handle.

Fold the thin card in half lengthways and crease. Open up and fold in half the other way. Open out again and fold in the two sides so, when opened, you have eight squares divided by crease lines. Cut down the middle crease line on either short side to the first fold line across (see diagram). Cut lengths of string or raffia 20 cm long and glue close together across the centre four squares. Paint brown (to resemble thatch). Glue one of the end squares over the other one at either end. Put glue on the outside of the bottom peak and glue this inside the box to make the roof of the house. Bend the 4×16 cm card into an open-ended cube and stick the two loose edges together with sticky tape. Paint to resemble a chimney: cut out triangular pieces on one end of two opposite sides and fit chimney over the roof. Place house in position on board.

Hay Barn

You will need:

Thick card, approx. 20×12 cm

Corrugated paper, approx. 20×20 cm

Glue, Scissors, Paints

What to do:

Cut the card into six strips 20×2 cm. Cut up 4 cm in the middle at one end of each strip and bend these tabs in opposite directions. Paint the strips and the corrugated paper in a rusty brown colour. When dry, roll the corrugated paper (corrugated side out) so that it naturally forms an arc shape. Glue the uncut strip at each end inside the corrugated paper—one at either end and one in the middle on opposite sides. Glue the tabs at the bottom of the strips to the farm board, so that the roof remains arched.

Hay Bales, Fences, Hedges and Trees

Stack some hay bales in the barn and make little ricks to stand in the fields with the others.

You will need:

Small matchboxes

Gold coloured wool

Glue

What to do:

Wind the wool round the matchboxes to completely cover them, so that they look like bales of hay! Dot with glue as you wind to keep the wool in place.

Put some fences round the farm to divide the fields.

You will need:

Plasticine

Cocktail sticks

Glue

What to do:

Decide where you want the fences to be. Press on little lumps of Plasticine along the ground line of the fence just under the length of a cocktail stick apart. Push a cocktail stick into each of these so that it stands upright. Glue two cocktail sticks horizontally between two vertical ones, about 3-4 cm apart, to make smart post and rail fencing.

If you prefer it, you could

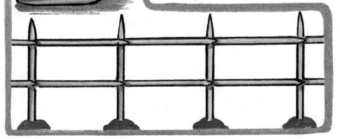

divide your fields with hedges.

You will need:

3 tablespoons of flour

3 teaspoons of salt

Cold water

Paints, Fork (or piece of stick)

Mix flour and salt together and add sufficient water to make a fairly stiff dough. Turn on to a floured board and knead the dough until it feels smooth and pliable. Roll into a long sausage, about 5 cm across and as long as you want the hedge to be. Press in place on the board and rough the top with a piece of stick or the prongs of a fork so it is not too smooth. When the dough is quite dry, paint it green.

Make a variety of trees to go round the farm.

A pine wood

You will need:

Tight fir cones

Plasticine

Green paint

What to do:

Select fir cones that have not opened out too much. Paint in varying shades of darkish green. When dry, press the bases into small lumps of Plasticine and group altogether on a corner of the board—where you want the wood to be.

Card trees

You will need:

Thin card, approx. 10×10 cm (for each tree)

Paint

Scissors

What to do:

Fold the card in half and draw the shape of half a tree top and trunk against the

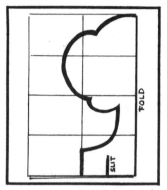

fold. Leave a piece at the bottom of the trunk (see diagram) and then cut out the outline and along the slits indicated. Paint the trunk and the foliage and bend the outer slits in the opposite direction to the middle one. Glue in place on the board.

Twiggy trees

You will need:

Small twig about 10 cm high with little branches growing off it
Green sticky paper
Scissors
Plasticine

What to do:

Cut individual leaves and clumps of leaves from the green paper and stick over the tree branches. Push the bottom into a lump of Plasticine so it stands up, and press the Plasticine into position by the pond.

Mr. and Mrs. Farmer

You will need:

3 pipe cleaners
Paper
Thick card
Scraps of felt or other non-fray fabric
Felt-tipped pens
Sticky tape

What to do:

Cut one pipe cleaner in half and bend each piece to form head and arms (see diagram). Bend the other two

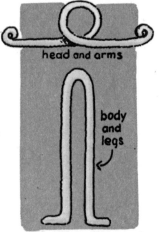

pipe cleaners in half, put the loop of each through the neck of the other pieces and then twist the ends round for about 4 cm to make the body. Bend 1 cm at the bottom of each 'leg' at right angles to the rest and tape to small pieces of thick card so the figures will stand up.

Cut out four circles from paper, the same size as the head loop (you could cut two of them with a hat

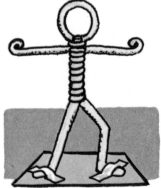

already on for Mr. Farmer). Draw face features on two of the circles and colour the other two brown for hair. Glue to either side of the pipe-cleaner head loops on each figure.

Mrs. Farmer: Cut out two dress shapes (see diagram)

from a scrap of fabric. Place a piece on either side of the Mrs. Farmer figure and over-sew along the shoulders and arms, and down the sides, with tiny stitches. Cut out a little white apron and stitch in place.

Mr. Farmer: Cut out smock and trouser shapes (see diagram). Sew on to model, catching smock to trousers at waist to keep in place.

Farm Animals

Cork sheep

You will need:
Old corks
Pins
Coloured card
Cotton wool
Glue, Scissors

What to do:
Stick four pins into one side of the cork at a slight angle to make legs. Cut an oval nose from coloured card. Mark in eyes with felt-tipped pens. Make a small slit at the top side of one end of the

cork and slot 'nose' in place. Glue cotton wool all over the back. Make several sheep and put them in a field.

Plasticine cows
You will need:
Plasticine
Used matchsticks
String
What to do:
Mould oval bodies of Plasticine. Stick in four used matchsticks to make legs and put a little piece of Plasticine on the end of each to make feet. Model small Plasticine heads. Break matchsticks into small pieces and use as 'necks' to join the head and body. You can also stick these little pieces into the head at either side to make horns. Stick on tiny pieces of frayed string as tails.

Potato pigs
You will need:
Small potatoes
Used matchsticks
Paper
Pins
Pipe cleaner
What to do:
Push four used matchsticks into one potato to make legs. Break another matchstick in half, push the two pieces into the 'head' potato (make sure it is smaller than the 'body'!) and push the two pieces into the body in such a way that the head is almost on the ground (to make your pigs look as if they are 'rooting' around). Cut two floppy ears from paper and push into the head with pins. Cut short length of pipe cleaner. Twist to make a curly tail and stick into the body.

N.B. As your pigs may appear rather large in proportion to the other farm animals, put them in a field at the front of the board.

Pipecleaner chickens
You will need:
Pipe cleaners
Red card
Paint
What to do:
Coil 15 cm length of pipe cleaner as shown. Paint yellowy brown. Cut out beaks and cocks' combs from red card and glue in place. Bend 6 cm length of pipe cleaner in half; push through the body coil to make legs. Bend ends to make feet so

chickens will stand. Put them round Mrs. Farmer in the yard.

Pebble ducks
You will need:
Small pebbles
Glue, Paint
What to do:
Select a smooth-bottomed pebble for duck's body. Glue on small ones to make head, wings and tail. When the glue is dry, paint yellow all over. Add a tiny orange beak and black eyes. Place on the pond.

Clay horses
You will need:
Self-hardening modelling clay
Recommended hardener
Small screwdriver
Paints, Varnish
What to do:
Mould a small piece of clay into the body shape, about 6 cm long (see diagram). Mould another piece into the head and neck shape (see diagram). Join these two pieces together by slightly dampening the end of the neck and pushing it on to the body. 'Stitch' the two pieces together with

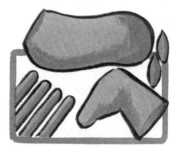

criss-cross cuts made with the screwdriver. Roll four bits of clay into sausages about 5 cm long and attach to the body as legs, in the same way. Flatten the other end so the horse stands easily. Stick on tiny ears and leave model to dry. Apply coats of hardener, following manufacturer's instructions. When quite dry, paint the horse brown. Glue on frayed string tail and mane and put in the yard near Mr. Farmer.

Flour-and-water dog and cat
Make a cat for Mrs. Farmer and a dog for Mr. Farmer.
You will need:
2 tablespoons flour
2 teaspoons salt
Cold water
Paints
What to do:
Make a flour-and-water dough, following the instructions for the hedge (see page 105). Model a little sitting cat and a dog, standing up, ready to obey his mas-

ter's command. Leave models to dry completely, then paint them, a black cat and a brown dog. Glue on tiny pieces of black and brown wool for tails.

All these basic modelling methods could be used to make any type of animal, and almost anything else you can think of! Try making your own zoo, or if you really want to let your imagination go, make a panorama of prehistoric monsters!

Cart for the Horse

You will need:
Inside part of a large matchbox
Thick cardboard
2 wooden ice-lolly sticks
Cotton
Glue, Paint, Scissors
What to do:
Cut out 'wheels' from the cardboard and glue to the lower part of the matchbox. Paint to look like a cart. Glue the lolly sticks on either side at one end as shafts. Tie a piece of cotton between the

sticks at the other end to go over the horse's back. Put in position behind horse in the yard.

Mr. Farmer's Car

You will need:
2 small boxes the same width (one needs to be taller than the other)
Thick card
Glue, Paint
What to do:
Glue the two boxes together as shown in the diagram.

Cut four circles from card. Paint to look like wheels and paint doors, windows and body of car. Glue wheels to the sides.

FUN WITH MAGIC

Here are some magic tricks to astonish your friends.

An Inside Job

Push a long, thin needle into a banana at three or four points along one of the seams. Then move it gently from side to side inside the skin. The pin holes won't show on the side, but when

you peel the banana, the flesh will fall into neat sections just as if it had been cut with a knife.

Rattle-Box

For this trick you must hide a matchbox holding a coin up your sleeve before you begin. Put three empty matchboxes on a table and put a coin in one of them. Shuffle the boxes around, keeping a check yourself which one contains the coin. Then pick up one of the *empty* ones and shake it. The matchbox up your sleeve will rattle, but your friends will think you are holding the matchbox with the coin. Put it back on the table and shuffle the boxes around (making sure your friends are watching closely). Then ask one of them to pick up the box with the coin in it. They will pick up the one you had before, and will wonder why it no longer rattles!

Pale-Fist

Give a friend a coin and turn your back. Ask her to hold it in one hand and to put that hand to her forehead while you are not looking. Then ask her to put both her clenched hands in front of her and you will say which one is holding the coin. You will be able to tell, because the hand that was held to the forehead will be paler than the other one.

GIVE A PARTY

Parties are fun! But it's not just going to them that's fun—it's giving them, too. There are lots of ways you can make your party special and memorable, and the planning and preparations beforehand are all part of the enjoyment.

Decide on a date with your mother and then plan how many people you would like to come. Don't be too ambitious—not too many people will give you more time to make sure everything is just right. If it is a 'special occasion' party, such as one given at Easter or Hallowe'en or Christmas or your birthday, you can make that the theme of the party. Then you can decorate the room and make food to fit in. For example, you could hide Easter eggs round the room and make an Easter cake for tea if it is an Easter party, or put up traditional Christmas decorations and make Christmas feast-time goodies if it is a Christmas party. But parties that you give at any old time just because you want to have a get-together with your friends are just as much fun.

The first thing to do is to send out invitations, and those you make yourself are the best of all. If it is a special occasion party you could obviously make your invitation to fit in with the theme—in the shape of a Christmas tree or Easter egg perhaps, or a black cat or witch's hat for Hallowe'en.

Here are two ideas for ordinary invitations.

Postcard Invitations
You will need:
> Plain postcards
> Coloured paper from old magazines
> Felt-tip pens
> Glue, scissors

How to make them:
Cut out some circles from the coloured paper. (You could draw round a 5-pence

piece.) Glue three or four onto the plain side of the card (see diagram) and draw in strings with a felt-tip pen to look like balloon strings.

Then write out your party message. It should say something like this:

> Dear Jane,
> I am having a party on 3rd August, starting at 3.00 in the afternoon. Please come if you can.
> > R.S.V.P. to:
> > Carol Smith
> > 31 Fern Lea Drive
> > Green Oaks.

Make an invitation for each of your friends in the same way. Write their names and addresses on the other side of the cards and send them off.

Easy-Reply Invitations
Here's an invitation which your friends can use to reply to you.

> You will need:
> Large sheet of white paper
> Felt-tip pens
> Pages from old magazines
> Envelopes
> Glue, Scissors

How to make them:

Cut out long strips of card and fold them, concertina-fashion, into three. (Make sure they fit into the envelopes.) On the front draw a pretty border with felt-tip pens and then cut out large letters from the magazines to make the words PARTY TIME! Glue them onto the card inside the border.

Write your party message across the inside double page. You could decorate it with a border again, or draw little pictures, or stick on pictures cut from the magazines.

Draw a dotted line along the final fold. Then write out:

My name is . . . .
I can come to your party—hooray!
I'm sorry I can't come to your party.

Add a note at the end saying: 'Please fill this part out and send it back to me, crossing out whichever is not applicable.'

Presents for the Guests

It is always nice to take away a small memento from a party, and things made by the hostess are especially pleasing. Little figures of animals make good, tiny presents for the guests. Here are a couple of ideas —can you think up some more?

Felt Animals

You will need:
Scraps of coloured felt
Oddments of wool and string
Cotton wool
Sewing thread, Needle
Glue

How to make them:

For each basic animal: Cut out three egg-shapes of felt, each about 5 cm long. Sew two together along the long edge and halfway down each shorter side. Open out and stitch the final shape to the sides. Leave a 3 cm gap

and push cotton wool into the figure to make it a nice, firm, even shape. Sew up the gap. Now you can sew on a variety of features to turn your basic shape into an animal. For example:

Cat: Make the basic shape in black felt. Cut out pointed ears and sew either side at the 'sharper' end. Embroider green eyes and sew fine string through the face for whiskers. A length of black wool stitched on to the back for a tail completes the cat!

Spotty Dog: Make a brown felt shape. Sew on floppy ears, embroider eyes and glue on a red felt tongue. Cut out small white felt circles and glue to the sides. Give it a string tail.

What other animals can you make from this shape? A mouse? A tiger? What else?

Bobbin People

You will need:
Empty cotton reels
Scraps of wool
Coloured card
Felt-tip pens
Glue, Scissors

How to make them:
Draw funny faces on the cotton reel with coloured pens, or glue on tiny felt features. Cut out feet and hand shapes in coloured card, following the patterns given.

Glue feet to base of cotton reels and hands to the sides. Cut wool into short lengths and glue to the top to make bushy hair.

Sweet Baskets for All

Make a personalised sweet basket for each guest.

You will need:
Cardboard tube (about 5-7 cm in diameter)
Strong paper, Thin card
Sticky labels
Glue, Paint, Scissors

How to make them:
Cut the cardboard tube into 5 cm lengths. Cut circles from the paper approximately 2 cm more in diameter than the tube. Make 1 cm cuts round the circle. Spread glue over these tabs, place the tube in the middle of the circle and glue tabs to the outside to make a base

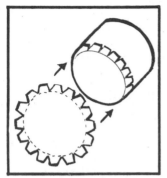

to the basket. Cut strips of thin cardboard, 1 cm wide and 10 cm long. Paint them and then glue either end each side of the top of the basket to make a handle. Cut strips of paper the same depth as the tube to go right round it and glue these in place. Paint the basket. Write the name of each of your guests on a sticky label and stick it to the outside of the basket. Fill each one with little sweets.

Party Food!

One of the greatest delights of parties is undoubtedly the party spread! An attractively set-out table almost groaning with delicious goodies is a sight almost everyone likes to see. Plan it well in advance with your mother, but you do as much of the preparation yourself as possible. (Always ask for help when cooking on the stove or using sharp knives.)

Savoury Ideas

All sorts of sandwiches

Ask a grown-up to cut off all the crusts from a loaf of bread and slice it lengthways into six slices.

Circle sandwiches: Spread two long slices with butter. Mash some sardines with a little lemon juice and spread all over one slice. Mix some cream cheese with chopped walnuts and spread over the other slice. Roll up each slice like a Swiss roll, wrap in foil and chill in the fridge. Before the party, cut the rolls into thin slices and arrange on plates with little flag labels stating the filling.

Triple deckers: Butter one side of the remaining slices. You can either make a savoury decker or a sweet decker. Either way you need three fillings to spread on the slices. Savoury ones could be cold scrambled egg mixed with mayonnaise, a layer of grated cheese mixed with tomato chutney and a layer of thinly sliced ham. Sweet ones could be a layer of mashed banana, a

115

layer of honey mixed with chopped nuts and a layer of thinly spread chocolate spread. Sandwich the layers together with the plain slice

on top. Chill and then slice as you would an ordinary loaf. Cut the sandwich slices into fingers, arrange on plates and label.

Sausage rolls: Thaw out a packet of flaky pastry and roll it into a long oblong about 10 cm wide. With floured hands shape a packet of sausage meat into a long thin sausage. Place this on the pastry, wet the edges and fold over the

sausage meat. Press the edges together. Cut the strip into individual rolls about 4 cm long. Make a diagonal cut across the top of each one and put them on a baking tray. Brush the top of each with a little milk. Ask a grown-up to bake them at 400°F or gas mark 6 for about 25-30 minutes.

Porcupine grapefruit: Drain the juice from a tin of pineapple chunks. Cut some hard cheese into small cubes. Spear a cheese cube and pineapple chunk with a cocktail stick and push into the skin of the grapefruit. Stick cocktail sticks all over it. Repeat with the second half of the grapefruit, but this time put a small pickled onion and cube of cheese on each cocktail stick.

Vol-au-vents: Scramble some eggs. Mix with tomato ketchup and chopped parsley. Fill little bought vol-au-vent cases (bite-size ones) with the mixture.

Sweet Things

Trifle: Make a big bowl of this delicious pudding. Cut a packet of trifle sponges in half and spread each piece with raspberry jam. Put them in the bottom of a glass dish. Open a can of mandarin oranges and one of cherries and sprinkle six tablespoons of the juices

over the sponges. Then put in most of the fruit from each can. Make up half pint of custard, following the directions on the packet. Pour it over the cakes and fruit. When the custard is cool, decorate the top with whipped cream, the remainder of the fruit and some pieces of angelica cut into diamond shapes.

Fairy cakes: Once you know how to make the basic mixture for fairy cakes you can vary it in endless ways. For the basic mixture you need:

    4 oz (113 grammes) of butter

    4 oz (113 grammes) caster sugar

    2 eggs

    4 oz (113 grammes) self-raising flour

Cream the butter and sugar together until they are pale and creamy (this will make your arm ache!). Beat the eggs with a fork and add a little at a time to the butter and sugar mixture, beating well all the time. Sieve the flour over the cake-mix bowl and fold (not beat) it into the mixture, using a metal spoon. Spoon the mixture into little cake cases and ask a grown-up to bake them at 350°F or gas mark 4 for about 20 minutes.

Variations and ways to decorate: When the cakes are cool, sieve some icing sugar and mix with a very little water to get a stiff cream mixture. Divide it into two bowls and put a few drops of red food colouring into one and a few drops of green into another. Drop a teaspoonful on to the centre of a cake and swirl it round with the underside of the teaspoon to coat the cake evenly. Top with coloured silver balls, hundreds and thousands or half a glacé cherry.

You can make chocolate butterfly buns by using 3 oz (85 grammes) of flour only and adding 1 oz (28 grammes) of cocoa. When the cakes are cold, cut off the top and cut this piece into

117

two. Make some butter icing by beating together 2 oz (56 grammes) butter and 2 oz (56 grammes) sieved icing sugar. Then beat in 1 oz (28 grammes) of chocolate powder. Spread a little of this on the top of each cake and push the two pieces into it to look like wings.

Make chocolate nutty buns by mixing in 2 oz (56 grammes) of chocolate polka dots and 2 oz (56 grammes) of chopped nuts with the flour. Decorate with chocolate butter icing and a chocolate button.

Cornflake crispies: Put some greased greaseproof paper on a baking tray. Put a pudding basin in a saucepan of hot—but not boiling —water. Break 6 oz (170 grammes) of chocolate into it and let it melt. Stir in cornflakes or Rice Krispies—enough to make a

nice, fairly solid, sticky lump! Using two teaspoons, spoon this in little dollops on to the baking tray and leave to harden.

Gingerbread men: These are great fun to make—and eat. First draw and cut out the gingerbread-man shape (see illustration) on to a piece of cardboard and cut it out. Then, with a grownup's help, heat 3 oz (85 grammes) of margarine with 2 tablespoonfuls of golden syrup and 2 oz (57 grammes) of sugar. Don't let them boil. Dissolve $\frac{1}{2}$ teaspoon of bicar-

bonate of soda in a little water and add this to the ingredients in the saucepan. Sieve in 7 oz (198 grammes) of flour and 1½ teaspoons of ground ginger and mix to form a dough. Cover the bowl with a clean tea cloth and leave for one hour. Roll out the dough so it is about 0.5 cm thick, then make gingerbread men by cutting round your cardboard shape. Ask a grown-up to bake them at 325°F or gas mark 3 for about 15 minutes.

These are just a few suggestions for party food, and you will be able to think of lots more. Mix up some nice jugs of orange and lemon squash before the party. Float a few slices of fruit in them and put them in the fridge, so they are nice and cold at teatime. Or make milk shakes by sieving a tin of raspberries or strawberries and whisking the purée with some milk. Just before serving, you could pop in spoonfuls of ice-cream.

Remember to wash up all your cooking utensils when you have finished. Dry them and put them away. Then wipe over all the surfaces in the kitchen where you have been working, so that it is clean and sparkling, just as it was when you began.

The Room

Make sure any valuable ornaments or vases are put out of the way, just in case of accidents. If you are having a lot of people, move out some of the smaller bits of furniture, too—you can always sit on the floor! You can decorate the room with paper streamers if you like, but lots of balloons blown up and hung from light fittings or picture hooks always make a room look ready for a party! Only hang pictures and posters on the wall if you have checked with your mother first. Anyway, it is best to glue them on to a large piece of cardboard and fasten some string to the back so you can hang them from a picture hook. Don't stick things directly on to the wall—it leaves nasty marks.

The Table

Lay the table for the number of guests you have coming. Give everybody a plate, a knife, a spoon and a glass. Fold one paper napkin into a pretty pattern for each place as well. Make a centrepiece

119

for the table. A maypole would be pretty and impressive!

Paint the outside of a cottage cheese or margarine tub (the larger sort) and fill it

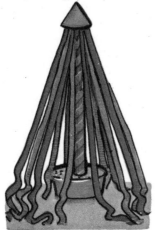

with sand. Cut strips of crêpe paper in two colours and wind them spirally round a long cardboard tube. Secure at the top and bottom with a spot of glue or sticky tape. Push the tube right down into the sand. Cut out long strips of crêpe paper in the two colours (you will need one strip for each guest) and stick them at one end round the top of the tube. Cut out a circle of stiff coloured paper and cut out a wedge from it. Twist the remainder into a cone and glue it to the top of the tube to hide the tops of the crêpe paper.

Make orange jelly boats

to go round the pole. Cut oranges in half (you will need one orange for every four guests). Scrape out all the juice and inside flesh and strain it to get rid of the pith. Use it to make up some orange jelly (follow the instructions on the packet). Leave it to cool and then pour a little into the orange halves. When it has set, cut each half in half again, using a knife dipped in hot water. Cut out square paper sails and write the name of each guest on them. Push a cocktail stick through the top and bottom to make a billowing spinnaker and push the bottom of this into the jelly. Top each stick with a

glacé cherry. Use clear tape to stick the ends of the crêpe paper strips to the bottom of each boat, and put in front of each guest's place so they can see where they are going to sit.

Arrange all the food attractively on plates and put them round the table. Fill a few dishes with potato crisps and peanuts and put them on the table, too.

Games to Play

Think up lots of games to play before the party, so you can be sure of keeping your guests entertained the whole time.

It is a good idea to have a sort of perpetual game going when people arrive because they can get to know each other (if they don't already) while you are busy greeting your other guests. You could glue pictures from magazines on to cardboard and then cut them into two, three or four pieces. Put all the bits in a box and then as each guest arrives she takes one. Then she has to find the people who have the rest of the pieces to make a complete picture.

Later on you can play team games or all-against-all games. Team games, which usually involve some activity, are probably best played before tea, and when you are all full-up you can play quieter, less energetic games. There are hundreds of different games to play at parties, and the fun thing is to try to think up new ones that no one has played before. Here are a few old favourites to get you into the party spirit.

Team Games

String Along: Divide your guests into teams. If there's an odd number, you be the umpire. Tie the ends of two pieces of string together to make two separate string circles. They should be just large enough to go over the widest part of the body. The teams stand in two long lines and the first person puts her arms through the string circle, pulls it over her head, down her body, and steps out of it. She passes it to the person behind her, who steps into it, pulls it up her body, and off over her head. The next person in the guests into two teams. Give each team a fan and a balloon. Players take it in turns to 'fan' the balloon up the room, round the chair and back to the others before handing the fan to the next team member, who does the same thing. Players must not touch the balloon with their fan—if they do they have to start again. Have a

line pulls it over her head and down her body, and so on to the end of the line. The last person holds up the string as soon as she has finished and her team is the winner.

Balloon Blowing: The room should be as clear as possible for this game with just two chairs at one end. Make two concertina fans out of newspaper and divide the

stock of un-blown-up balloons ready. If a player bursts the balloon she is given a new one which she must blow up then and there before she can continue the game.

All-Against-All Games

Mad Hatters: Give all your guests a large sheet of newspaper and some pins. Then give them five minutes to make a hat. At the end of the time they must all model their creation in front of everybody. Ask a grown-up to choose which is the best, and you could give the winner a small prize.

Chinese Whispers: No one wins or loses this game; it's just a very funny one to play! Sit everybody in a circle on the floor. Think up a simple sentence like 'Bees make lovely honey' or 'I saw Sue at the bus stop.' Whisper it to the person next to you, quite quickly. She must then whisper it to the person next to her, and so on round the circle. The last person says out loud what she thinks the person before her said. It is usually quite different from the original!

Now think up some more games for your party!

A Good Idea

Although parties are primarily for you and your friends to have fun, towards the end, and while you have all your friends together, why not spend a few minutes thinking of things you can do to help other people —either together or in smaller groups. Maybe someone will know an old lady who lives on her own and would welcome some company now and again, perhaps to give her a hand with the gardening. Or maybe there's somebody else who is not well and would appreciate someone to do her shopping or help her with the housework. Or perhaps you could think up some things to make together for the next 'good cause' fête or bazaar. Maybe think of one way in which you can all help in your own home for the next week (yours will start right after the party when you help your mother to clear up!). Such things become fun when they are planned, or carried out, together, and it turns your party into something that will give pleasure to other people, too.

INDOOR GARDENING

Bulbs For Indoors

Spring bulbs—daffodils, hyacinths, crocuses and tulips—bring a lovely breath of spring air into the house after the long winter months, and they are easy to grow.

You can grow hyacinth bulbs in jam jars. Choose a jar which the bulb fits into, resting around the brim without falling into the bottom. Put a few pieces of charcoal in the bottom of the jar and then fill it up with water so that it just touches the bottom of the bulb, when you place this on top. Put the jar into a darkened cupboard and leave it for about eight weeks. By this time the roots will be growing down, and you must make sure there is now some air space between the water and the bottom of the bulb, or else it will rot. When a shoot appears and is well formed, you can bring the jar out into the open—and wait for it to flower!

Another way of growing bulbs is to fill pretty bowls or containers with bulb fibre and plant the bulbs in them. Plant hyacinths and daffodils so their 'noses' are just visible, tulips so they are just covered, and crocuses so their tips are about 1 cm beneath the surface of the fibre. Make sure the bulbs do not touch each other and the fibre is moist. Then put them away into a darkened cupboard, checking from time to time that the fibre is still moist. When the shoots appear and are quite well formed, you can bring them out into the open, ready to burst forth into a lovely spring show!

Indoor Vegetables and Fruit Trees

You can grow mustard and cress seeds on saucers and dishes indoors. Cut a piece of lint or flannel to fit in the dish and soak it in water. Sprinkle the seeds over it and place the dish by a sunny window. Keep the fabric continually moist and you will be able to cut the green tops off in just a few weeks' time. Lovely for salads and sandwiches.

Another way of growing cress is in an empty yogurt pot or cream carton. Scrub it first to remove the writing and then draw a funny face with felt-tip pens on the outside. Half fill it with small pebbles, then top it up with moist soil and sprinkle the seeds on the top. After a little while your funny face will have grown a mop of green hair!

Fruit pips will grow into lovely little indoor trees if you look after them carefully. Choose really plump pips from oranges, lemons, grapefruits or tangerines and soak them for a day in cold water. Put a layer of pebbles in the bottom of a flower-pot and then fill it up with a commercial potting compost—well dampened. Plant two or three pips 1-2 cm beneath the surface of the compost and then either cover the top of the pot with a large glass jam jar or a polythene bag supported on four sticks pushed into the soil round the edge of the pot. Tie the bottom of the bag round the top of the flower-pot. This helps to create a humid atmosphere which the pips need to start growing.

Put the flower-pot in a dark place until little shoots begin to appear. Then remove the jar or bag, and as soon as each tiny plant has two leaves on it replant them in individual pots and transfer them to a light, warm place. Keep them watered and they will grow into pretty little trees.

A Bottle Garden

Growing your own bottle garden is a lovely way of having plants indoors the whole year round. In fact, once established, they will last for several years with very little care and attention.

You can buy bottle gardens in florists, but they are very expensive, and it is quite easy to make one yourself. It would make a nice present for someone, maybe an elderly person who lives on their own in a flat.

First of all you need a large jar. A squarish sweet jar from a sweet shop is ideal, as it can be laid on its side and has a nice wide neck which makes the initial planting easier.

Make yourself some bottle garden tools; you will need a 'trowel', a 'fork' and a 'soil rammer'. Tie an old teaspoon and fork to lengths of bamboo for the trowel and fork, and for the rammer, push a length of bamboo into an empty cotton reel, first smearing glue round the top to secure it.

Wash the bottle and dry it out thoroughly. Lay it on its side and put in a layer of tiny pebbles mixed with charcoal. Then spoon in a layer of moist potting compost so it is about 5-7cm deep (don't use garden soil, it will be full of weed seeds). If there are any bits of soil sticking to the sides and top of the bottle, sponge them off carefully with a spongy washing-up mop.

You will probably have to

buy the plants, but as you only need very small ones, they shouldn't be too expensive. Ones that grow too quickly or overpoweringly are not good to use as they will soon swamp everything else. Foliage plants are better than flowering ones and some good ones are: *Helxine solerrolii* (Mind Your Own Business), *Marantas* (Prayer Plant), *Pilea cadierei* (Friendship Plant), *Fittonia verschaffeltii* (Snakeskin Plant), *Calatheas* (Peacock Plant), and *Cryptanthus bivittatus* (Starfish Plant). Learn to use their Latin

Water the plants using a small garden spray and then screw the lid on the jar. From then on you will need to water the bottle only every six to eight months. For the first few days each time, a layer of condensation will probably form round the sides, but this soon disappears. Keep the bottle garden in a place which gets good light, but avoid direct sunlight as this will scorch the plants.

Arranging Flowers

Besides growing bulbs and flowers indoors, it is nice to have cut flowers arranged in vases from time to time. They especially help to cheer up an invalid's room. Learn how to arrange flowers so they look at their best; it's not necessary to have masses and masses; how you put them in a vase is the important thing.

Choose the vase carefully for the flowers. Don't use a tall one for short flowers, so the heads just peep over the top! As a guide, the tallest flowers should be about one and a half times the height of the vase.

If you are using roses in your arrangements, cut the stems up the middle for about 3 cm. Crush the stems of woody plants like lilac with a hammer and just cut

names; it is how florists identify them and it avoids the confusion that often occurs if you use their common names.

Planting can take a little practice, so be patient. Make little holes in the soil with the trowel and push in your plants with the fork. Spread out the roots as much as possible, still using the fork, and then rake soil over them. Firm the soil down with the rammer. Then firm the compost with the rammer so there are no gaps between it and the roots of the plants.

the stems of other flowers on a slant to open them up as much as possible. Steep the flowers in cold water which comes two-thirds of the way up their stems before arranging them.

Chicken wire or florists' wire put into a vase will help shape of the arrangement. Fill it out and down to the sides and front, using the shorter flowers, cutting them to size where necessary. Fill in the gaps, still keeping the outline of the shape, using the flowers and foliage you have selected.

to keep the flowers where you want them. Place it in the vase and top up with cold water. Then take off the leaves and branches that will come below the water in the vase, as they will rot, making the water slimy and stagnant.

If you are doing an arrangement that will be placed against a wall, put the tallest flowers at the back and start by making a basic framework for the

If you are doing a small circular or oval arrangement for a table, remember it has to look nice from all sides. Put the tallest flowers in the middle of the vase (it is likely to be considerably shallower than the one you used for a 'facing' arrangement) and then build the shape outwards on all sides from there. The flowers and foliage should cover the edges of the vase, too.

Outdoors

In the Country

WALKS AND RAMBLES

Preparing For a Walk

If you're going for a long walk, you can avoid getting sore feet and blisters (which make you miserable and ruin your walk!) by rubbing

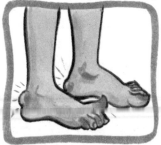

surgical spirit on to your feet for a week or so beforehand. It helps to harden the skin. Always wear comfortable, tough shoes for walking, not wellington boots or sandals, which soon get uncomfortable if you walk for long. Thick socks rather than thin, skimpy ones will be more comfortable too.

Again, if you're going for a very long walk, an older friend or grown-up may be coming with you and can help you to plan a route on a

large scale map. Map reading is interesting, but can be quite hard to do until you get the hang of it. Ask them to help you follow a route you know on a map—either a country walk across fields and woods you're familiar with, or perhaps your route to school on a street map of your town. Either way, you'll begin to get familiar with map reading, and can then plan a long ramble on your own or with friends of your own age.

Although map reading may

take a little while to master, you can learn to use a compass quite easily in the meantime, and this is very useful in helping you to find your way to and from places.

Going for long walks in

the country is one of the great pleasures in life and something nearly everybody can enjoy. Don't think because you live in the middle of a town, this is a pastime which you can't do —because you can. No town is more than a bus ride away from fields and woods, but going for long walks around your home town can be just as much fun and if you are observant you'll learn all sorts of new things about the place where you live. The time when you have the greatest opportunity for a country ramble is if you go on a camping holiday with your parents or some older friends or relatives.

Which Way is North?

A compass has eight points. Reading clockwise, they are North, North-East, East, South-East, South, South-West, West and North-West.

If you hold it flat on your hand, or better still on a map, the needle will swing round to point to north, so you can then work out the directions of south, east and west and the points between them.

Use a compass to find out which way your bedroom faces. Is your school north or south of your home? Work out where places you know are in relation to where you live, so that you really get to know how to use a compass. Then when you go for walks, knowing, or being able to work out, the direction of your home from where you are will always help you to find your way back, should you get lost.

If you have no compass, you can work out where north is from the position of the sun. It rises in the east and sets in the west. At noon, when it is at its highest point in the sky, it is due south, so in the morning it is between east and south, and in the afternoon it is between south and west. Learn to recognise where the sun is in the sky when you are out walking.

Make-a-Map

Make a map of the streets around your home; it will help you to understand, and

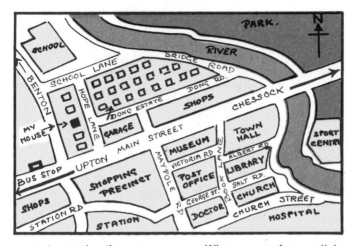

soon to read, other maps. Make it a large-scale one—perhaps 10 cm to 1 km—and try to keep it all in scale. Draw in all the roads around you. Write in their names and put direction arrows at the sides of the map showing the names of the places the different roads lead to. Then mark in your home, the nearest bus stop, your school, the post office, the town hall, the church, any historic buildings or museums, the library, the garage, the doctor's surgery; just anything you can think of and would like to include! Is there a river or a stream in your town? Mark it on the map in blue crayon and show where there's a bridge over it. Work out which way is north on your map and mark that on, too.

When you go for a walk in the country, make a map when you get home showing where you've been. Use the recognised signs to indicate the different things you passed on your walk. These are the ones used on Ordnance Survey maps, and you should get to know what they mean.

Did you spot a rabbit or a bird you recognised; some wood pigeons or a black-bird, perhaps? Or maybe even a squirrel? Mark the spot where you saw them on your map and write it in. It makes for an interesting map, and will help you to remember that walk later.

Things to Do on Town Walks

Use your walks to find out more about the town or village where you live. Go inside the church and read the plaques on the wall. Find out when it was built and what the town was like then. The local library (or museum if there is one) will probably be a good source for finding out about your town's history. They may even have some old maps of the area which are great fun to look at and compare with the present-day one. Perhaps the street names have been changed, or maybe, on the spot where your school now stands, for example, there used to be a farm! Compare the places you know with those on the old map.

Find out as much as you can about the old buildings you see as you walk by. When were they built? Sometimes they have plaques on the wall giving the name of some famous person who used to live there.

Find out why he or she was famous. Take a sketch pad with you on your walks and make sketches of the different types of buildings you see. Perhaps there are some

ruins of an old castle or abbey nearby. See if you can discover the part it played in history, and when it became a ruin. Finding out all these things will give you a much greater appreciation of the things around you, as well as making your walks, and you, more interesting!

Things to Do on Country Walks
Take a pocket book on trees and wild flowers with you and use it to identify those you see. Some of the more common trees and wild flowers found in this country are illustrated opposite. Learn to recognise trees by shape, in summer and winter, as well as by leaves.

Keep your eyes skinned as you walk along for wild animals such as rabbits, hares, squirrels and field mice. If you're very lucky you may see a fox. Even if you don't actually see any animals at all, look out for their footprints on soft woodland or meadow tracks. Look in reference books for information on the wild animals of Britain, illustrated with their different footprints or 'spoors', as they are called.

Look out for birds, too, and make a note of those you see. Then when you get home you can find out more

Daisies and Buttercups

Larch

Bluebell

Horse Chestnut

about them; where they live, what kind of nest they build, the colour of the eggs they lay. In springtime, you might find a nest in the low branches of a tree, or tucked into a hedgerow. Never disturb it, or take away any of the eggs; just look very quietly and see if you can tell which bird has made it by the shape of the nest or the colour of the eggs, if there are any.

Remember the Country Code whenever you are walking:

⚹ ALWAYS SHUT GATES BEHIND YOU (TYING THEM UP IF NECESSARY)
⚹ NEVER LEAVE LITTER BEHIND—ANYWHERE
⚹ KEEP TO RECOGNISED PATHS AND TRACKS ACROSS FARMLAND

135

- DON'T DAMAGE TREES IN ANY WAY. NEVER PULL UP WILD FLOWERS BY THE ROOTS
- ONLY PICK A FEW OF ANY ONE TYPE OF FLOWER AND NONE AT ALL OF RARE SPECIES
- MAKE SURE YOU DON'T DAMAGE WALLS, FENCES AND HEDGES
- IF YOU HAVE A DOG WITH YOU, KEEP IT UNDER CONTROL. BE PARTICULARLY CAREFUL IN FIELDS WHERE FARM ANIMALS ARE GRAZING.

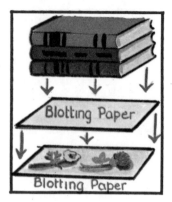

Collections

You could make a collection of leaves and wild flowers from those you find on your walk. Particularly with flowers, read about them first and if they are rare, don't pick them at all. It's all right to pick a few flowers of the commoner types, but never pull up a root, and only take one or two flowers.

You can press both leaves and flowers when you get home, thus making a permanent collection as a reminder of your country walks. Choose the best specimens of each and lay them out on a sheet of newspaper or blotting paper, so they don't touch one another. With flowers such as violets, daisies and primroses, arrange the petals in their natural circle, as flat as possible and facing upwards. Put foxgloves, clover and similar flowers on their side. You can leave buttercups on their stems in sprays, either laying the petals flat to show an open flower or folded to look like a closed one. Cover with another sheet of newspaper or blotting paper and then put a heavy pile of books on top.

Leaves and flattish sorts of flowers should be ready in a couple of weeks or so; fleshy flowers will need a little longer. Once they are all quite dry and stiff, paste them into a scrapbook. Write their names and where and when you picked them by the side of them.

Other things you could collect on country walks are interesting stones and pebbles, fir cones and feathers. Wash the stones and pebbles and keep them in a glass jar filled with water (it will make them shiny). Larger ones you could paint and varnish and make into paperweights. Find out which tree your fir cones came from. Then glue them on to empty cotton reels to make a fir-cone forest. Write the names of the trees on sticky labels and stick them to the cotton reels. See if you can discover which birds the feathers you find belonged to. Stick the feathers into an album and draw a picture of the bird by the side of them.

What other nature objects can you think of to collect? Think of ways to display your collection.

ROAD SAFETY

The dos and don'ts of road safety, whether you are a pedestrian or a cyclist, should be second nature to you. Make sure you know all the rules by heart and **always** practise them. Remember no two roads are ever quite the same, so you must always be thinking and on your guard. Never play games, particularly ball games, beside a road.

On the next page there is a selection of road signs in common use throughout this country. Make sure you know what they mean and the significance they hold for you. For example, if you are riding your bike, it is no good just knowing that a broken circle means there is a roundabout ahead. You must also know what precautions to take and the proper way to ride your bike around a roundabout.

Peacock

137

Stop and
give way

Give way to
traffic on
major road

No entry

School
crossing patrol

No right
turn

No left
turn

No cycling or
moped-riding

No pedestrians

Ahead
only

Turn left ahead
(Right if symbol
reversed)

Turn left ahead
(Right if symbol
reversed)

Route for
cyclists and
moped riders
(compulsory)

Road Rules For Pedestrians

1. Always use pavements and footpaths whenever they are there. Walk as far from the traffic as possible, not right on the kerb. Look both ways before you step into the road.

2. When there is no footpath, walk on the right-hand side of the road, facing the oncoming traffic and keeping as far off the road as possible. Never walk more than two abreast and take extra care round right-hand bends (it's best to keep one behind another here if possible).

3. If you have a small child or a dog with you, keep between them and the traffic. Don't let them run into the road. Hold the child's hand and keep your dog on a lead. You should never let your dog out on its own.

4. If it is dark or dusk,

wear or carry something white. Motorists will be able to see you earlier.

5. Always follow the Green Cross Code crossing a road. In other words, stop on the kerb, look right, look left, look right again. Listen as well as look. If the road is clear, **walk** (don't run) quickly across the road, still keeping a look-out for traffic. Do your kerb drill even in one-way streets and make sure you know which way the traffic is moving.

6. Always cross at pedestrian or zebra crossings, traffic lights, subways or footbridges if they are there. In the absence of these, cross where there are central islands, crossing the first half of the road to the island and making sure the road is clear before crossing the second half. If there is no island, always cross at a place where you can see clearly both ways. Never cross at guard rails (don't walk outside them either).

7. Remember, at zebra crossings you have no priority over traffic until you are actually on the road. But don't just step out on to it regardless —motorists need plenty

of space and time to stop. Even when one has stopped for you, still look left and right as you cross, because another motorist coming up behind might not have seen you. If there is an island in the middle of the crossing, use each half of the road as a separate crossing.

8. Try not to cross the road between, or in front of, parked vehicles, because drivers on the road might not be able to see you. If you have to cross near parked vehicles, stop at the edge of them and do your kerb drill.

9. If you are crossing at a road junction, look out for traffic turning the corner, especially beyond you.

10. At traffic lights, watch the traffic as well as the lights. At push-button-controlled crossings, wait for the signal to cross, even if the road is clear. Only cross when the green man is lit up; if it is flashing, don't cross.

11. If you are catching a bus, only get on, or off, if it is stationary at a recognised bus stop. If you want to cross the road after you have got off, wait until the bus has moved off so you have a clear view of the road.

Special Points For Cyclists
Before you take your bike on the road, make sure you are really proficient at riding it; that you can stop quickly whenever you want to; that you can take one hand off the handlebars to make a signal without wobbling all

over the place; and that you know the rules of the road. Never ride a bike that is too big for you—you should be able to put your feet on the ground on either side without straining. Also make sure your bicycle is in good condition with the brakes, lamps and rear reflector in working order, before you ride it.

1. Do not start off, turn right or left or pull up without first glancing behind you to see it is safe. Give clear signals to show what you intend to do.

2. Never ride more than two abreast; on busy or narrow roads, it is best to ride in single file. Generally when you want to turn right, you should signal and move over to the right of the road. On busy roads, however, it is often better to pull into the left side and wait for a safe gap in the traffic, in both directions, before starting to cross.

3. Always keep your hands on the handlebars and your feet on the pedals. Don't carry a passenger, unless your cycle

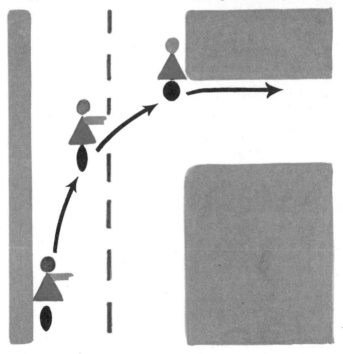

has been built or altered to carry one, and never carry anything which affects your balance. Don't ride close behind another vehicle and never hold on to a vehicle or another cyclist. Don't lead an animal from a bicycle.

4. If there is a cycle path beside the road, or a route especially designated for cycles and mopeds, make sure you use it.

Looking After Your Bicycle
Like most other things, a bicycle will last longer and work better if it is well looked after. Try and keep it in a damp-proof shed, for example, where it is less likely to rust. Keep it clean by wiping over all the chrome and metal parts regularly. If you have been riding along wet and muddy roads, you may need to wash it over, but dry it too, afterwards, to help prevent rust forming.

Although you should keep your bike looking clean and bright, it is even more important to make sure it is in perfect working order all the time. Use a recommended bicycle oil and oil the hubs of the wheels from time to time. (There are special holes

where you apply the oil.) Tilt the bike from side to side when you do this, so that the oil runs to both sets of bearings, but be careful not to use too much oil. It shouldn't ooze out and run down the spokes. If it does, wipe it off because it will damage the tyres.

Make sure the pedals are secure and oil their joints from time to time, too.

The chain is an extremely important part of your bike. Without it the bike just won't work. If you neglect it, it will break sooner or later—probably at the most awkward time possible, or when you are miles away from home. Brush all round the chain with a stiff brush to remove the dirt from between the rollers and then run some thick oil along the rollers. Turn the pedals a few times to disperse the oil well round the chain.

To put on a new chain, fit it first on to the smaller back wheel. Then place it over the first two cogs of the larger

front wheel, and wind it on by pushing the pedals round.

Oil round the brake fittings and cables, and gear levers, if your bike has them, as all these places are likely to go rusty and then won't work properly.

Get somebody who knows about bikes to help you check your brakes from time to time, because it is very important that these are working well. The rubber of rim brakes, in particular, wears down fairly quickly, and must then be replaced.

Pumping up tyres can be a boring job—much easier, isn't it, to ride your bike anyway, even if they are not quite as hard as they should be? Much easier—and much more likely to wear out your tyres quickly and get punctures. Tyres should always be pumped up so

hard that you can hardly make any impression on them with your thumb. Check round the tyres from time to time to make sure no tiny pebbles are lodged between the grooves of the tread. If they are left, they eventually force themselves through the tyres to puncture the inner tube. Your care will pay dividends!

GROWING THINGS

You don't need a huge garden to be able to grow flowers and vegetables—in fact you can still grow them if you haven't got a garden at all! If you have a tiny patch of ground you are allowed to use, you can grow all sorts of things; otherwise you can use a window box or even a saucer and a dish. You can also grow lovely gardens in bottles. (See pages 125-27.)

Doing simple gardening jobs is a good way to help other people. You could help to tidy somebody's garden by sweeping the paths and weeding the flower-beds, for example, but make sure you know which are weeds and which are flowers, or your help might not be appreciated! Remember to put all the gardening tools away after you have used them (forks and spades with their prongs and blades facing downwards, brooms with their bristles at the top), and scrape off any clods of earth still sticking to them before you put them away.

Grow a Salad

Buy packets of lettuce and radish seed and grow them for fresh crisp salads. You can plant the first lot of seeds in March, using about one-quarter of the packet. Then plant the remainder at fortnightly intervals so you don't get a huge glut of vegetables all at once.

If you are growing them in the garden, first dig over the ground with a fork to break up the earth. Remove all the weeds and rake over the patch so it is flat and even. Then dig narrow drills in the soil, about 2 cm wide and 1 cm deep and sow the seeds **thinly** along the row. Cover with a light smattering of soil and give them some water.

Water the seedlings as they appear, and when they have grown into little plantlets of about 4-5 cm high, you must transplant them. Prepare another patch of ground to make it flat and

even, then dig little holes about 25 cm apart in rows 20-25 cm apart. Dig up a trowelful of plantlets, separate them from each other and plant each one in the holes you have dug. Water them well all the time they are growing, otherwise the radishes will be very hot to eat and the lettuces will 'bolt' or go to seed, which means they grow straight

A Bolted Lettuce

upwards instead of developing nice, plump hearts inside.

You can see when the lettuces are ready for pulling up and eating, but keep a check on the radishes by pulling one up after a few weeks. Don't let them get too big before eating them.

If there isn't a patch of land you can use, sow your lettuce and radish seeds in some seed trays and when they are big enough transplant them into a window box. Put a layer of pebbles or broken flower-pots into the box to help drain and aerate the soil, then fill it with a layer of soil and potting compost mixed together. Remember to water your plants well all the time they are growing.

Both lettuces and radishes like nice, open, sunny positions.

More Window-Box Growing
Flowers grown in window boxes look pretty and bright. Choose ones that don't grow too tall—marigolds and nasturtiums are good because they are small and grow easily but they are bright and colourful.

You could also grow outdoor bulbs such as hyacinths or dwarf tulips. Remember to put pebbles or

crocks into the bottom of the box, and if you are growing bulbs, mix the soil with some peat. Bulbs are usually planted in the late autumn

145

for a lovely fresh spring show.

Window boxes are ideal places for growing a herb garden. Plant some thyme, parsley, chives and sage seeds into seed boxes in

Thyme

March or April. (Parsley seeds often take a long time to germinate—a good tip to speed them up is to pour boiling water over the seeds when you have sown them.) When the seedlings have grown into little plants, transplant them into your window box. You could include mint in your herb garden, too, but grow it in its

Mint

own flower-pot, and 'plant' the flower-pot into the soil of the window box. This is because mint grows and grows, overpowering everything around it. If you let it, it will soon take over your window box completely, but if you keep it in a pot, it is contined to its own small area.

ANIMAL CARE
Wild Animals

Generally speaking, keeping wild animals is far less satisfactory than keeping animals that have been bred as domestic pets. There are many cases, some famous, of people keeping foxes, otters and badgers, and even more extreme wild animals, such as lions, crocodiles and elephants, as pets, but for the average person it is not really advisable! A lion in your back garden may make you less than popular with your neighbours, and you might find yourself rather short of friends! In any event, these animals have evolved over the centuries to complete adaptation to life in the wild, and trying to tame them as pets brings its own massive problems.

Something you can easily do is attract wild birds to your garden, not so much to keep as pets, but to observe and get to know a little. Perhaps your father would

help you to construct a simple bird table at the top of a tall pole (make sure it is out of 'cat-reach'). On it you can put odd scraps from leftover meals, bacon rinds, bits of bread and so on. Hang monkey nuts and pieces of fat from bits of string; smaller birds such as tits will love them and keep you amused with their acrobatic antics. You could put an old pie dish nearby full of water and the birds will use it to take a 'bath', which can also be very entertaining.

If you make sure your bird table is always well stocked with scraps, you will soon recognise the same birds returning. Keep a record of the different birds that come to your garden; draw pictures of them and write down when you saw them, what they like to eat best and how they bathe.

Tadpoles that develop into frogs are more wild animals you can keep, for a while at least. Collect some frog spawn—that floating mass of jelly with black dots in it—from a pond in springtime. Keep it in a large glass bowl with some pond weed and watch the tadpoles grow and develop. You will have to feed the developing tadpoles on small scraps of meat or fish, and when they change into tiny frogs, return them close to the pond where you found them.

You can also keep lizards or toads or small grass snakes in a 'vivarium'. This is a glass-sided container similar in structure to an aquarium, but not filled with water! Instead put a layer of pebbles in the bottom and cover this with a layer of soil, unevenly distributed. Put in a few rocks and twigs and plant some plants. Put in a shallow container for water and then pop in your

147

toads, lizards or snakes. They will need scraps of coarse fish and tiny bits of raw meat, as well as small insects, grubs and worms. To prevent mishaps, cover the top with a sheet of fine wire gauze. If your animals show signs of misery or lethargy, it is best to return them to the wild.

One species of wild animal that is easily tamed and does make a good pet is the hedgehog. Not very often seen, it belongs to the same order of animals as shrews and moles.

The best time to catch hedgehogs is at dusk when they are at their most active. Wear thick gloves, or use a folded cloth to pick them up, but don't try to get hold of them or pick them up by their spines. When you first catch one, it will be very shy, and curl up into a ball every time you come near, so you will have to put down its food and then watch from a little way off. Soon it will get used to you, however, and you'll probably be able to feed it from your hand.

Keep your hedgehog in a large pen made of wire netting with 1 cm-wide holes. Since it is a good burrower and climber, dig your netting 20 cm or so into the ground and cover the top of the pen with it as well.

Give it a little wooden box as a bedding place, with a doorway in one side, and line it with dry hay or leaves. Besides sleeping every day

in this, the hedgehog will probably go into it in late autumn and stay there through its winter hibernation. You should leave it alone at this time, but if it wakes up, as it may do on a sunny day, give it a feed.

A hedgehog's diet consists of worms, slugs and beetles, which you must provide for it. It will also like an occasional feed of tinned dog food and root vegetables. As with all animals, make sure it always has fresh water available.

As hedgehogs are nearly always infested with fleas and ticks, it is a good idea to get some insecticide powder from your vet to try to minimize the problem. Change the bedding frequently, as that will also help to control fleas.

A PET OF YOUR OWN

Having a pet of your own, whether it's a cat or a dog or a goldfish or a hedgehog that's wandered into the garden, is something very special. But because animals are living, breathing beings with feelings and miseries just like us, you must think very carefully before you become a pet owner. After all, the responsibility for the happiness and health of your pet will be entirely in your hands. Think how much time you have to look after it; whether you have a reliable friend who can look after it should you go away at any time; how much you can afford to spend, both to obtain it and to feed and care for it afterwards. There will be vets' bills to consider, too; animals get sick just the way we do, and vets' bills can be high. In addition, and very important, how much space do you have for pet keeping? It's no good having a large, high-spirited dog if you live on the top floor of a block of flats in the middle of a town, for example. In such a case it would be better to have a goldfish or a budgerigar; animals that don't rely on you to give them exercise.

When you have considered all these things, find out all you can about different sorts of pets, particularly the one you have in mind. Find out how to look after them, what they like to eat, what their habits are, and check this *before* you bring a pet home. (Make sure, too, to check with your parents that it is all right for you to keep a pet, anyway!)

And a final word. If your pet gets ill or injured, take it to the vet straight away. Don't imagine you can treat it yourself; you may actually do more harm than good. Keep the vet's name and address and phone number in a readily accessible place, and if you have entrusted your pet to someone else's care while you are on holiday, make sure they know all this information, too.

Cats

Cats are favourite pets and in many ways are easier to keep than dogs. In general they need less attention as they tend to be more independent and don't need to be taken out for walks.

Kittens are ready to leave their mother at about eight weeks old, and all you have to do is decide whether you want a male or a female. In either case it's best to have them neutered (the operation is done when a male is three months old, and when a female is four to five months old). If you want your cat to have kittens, and you are sure you can find homes for them all, then have a female (and don't have her neutered straight away), but remember cats can, and are likely to, have kittens twice a year!

Eight-week-old kittens must be injected by a vet against feline enteritis or distemper. Two injections are needed, the second a fortnight after the first.

When a kitten leaves its mother it will need four tiny meals a day. When they get to three months old they can have three meals. At seven months they only need two meals, and once they are ten

itself, it's probably not well, unless it is just a very lazy cat, and should be taken to the vet.

Provide your cat with a box or basket to sleep in, and put in an old warm blanket or the like. This will need washing regularly. If your cat can't get outside whenever it wants to, make a dirt tray for it inside. This is just a flat wooden box filled with cat litter, sand, ashes or earth.

months, and just about fully grown, they will only need one meal a day, of 120-170 grammes (4-6 oz). Cats like raw red meat and offal (liver and kidneys), which should be chopped up small. You can vary their diet by giving them fish and chopped chicken from time to time, but always make sure you have removed all the bones. Tinned cat foods are very good, but try different brands, and try to intersperse tinned meats with fresh food now and again. We all know that cats like saucers of milk, but make sure there is a bowl of fresh water available, too.

Cats are incredibly clean animals and will wash themselves scrupulously, so they need little grooming. It is quite a good idea to brush them when they are moulting as they might otherwise swallow the loose hairs when they lick themselves. If your cat is not cleaning

If you wrap a piece of sacking round one of the kitchen-table legs, or round a log, there's just a chance that your cat might use it to sharpen up or wear down its claws. This might save the best armchair which it will doubtless otherwise use!

Remember that although cats are independent animals, they do like some human attention apart from just being fed. Stroking them, scratching them behind the ears or whatever, is likely to bring a rewarding, responsive purr and will help to increase the trust and friendship between you.

Particularly if you are keeping a cat in a town, buy it a cat collar; make sure it is a proper one which will be made partly of wide elastic, so that if it gets caught on the branch of a tree the cat can escape. You can write your name and address on the collar, so people will know where to return the cat should it stray.

Dogs

There is much more to think about if your pet is to be a dog. First you must think what size it should be, and this will depend on the size of your home, how much you can afford to feed it and how much time you have to exercise it each day. As a general rule keep little dogs for town life; big dogs for the country. Little dogs will cost about £1 per week to feed; big dogs will cost upwards of £2. Little dogs ideally need two shortish walks a day, but these could just be round the local street, while big dogs can need as much as a ten-kilometre walk a day, ideally where they can work off their surplus energy by bounding through woods or heathland. So it is the size and not a special sort of

OLD ENGLISH SHEEPDOG

BOXER

breed that should initially govern your choice of dog.

There are so many different types of breed that to describe each of them would take another whole book. So having decided on the size that is best for you, read about the breeds for yourself. Some suitable small breeds are small spaniels, dachshunds, poodles, terriers (although

many are very yappy and some need more exercise than most small dogs) and pekineses. Larger breeds include dalmatians, setters, Old English sheepdogs, labradors and boxers. The last two are particularly good with children, but labradors need a lot of exercise if they are not to become too fat. Don't discount the idea of a mongrel; they come in all shapes and sizes and are usually very good-tempered and affectionate.

It's best to take someone who knows about dogs with you when you go to choose one. If that's not possible, check the following things yourself: its *nose* should be clean, damp and cold; its *breath* should not smell unpleasant; its *coat* should be glossy with loose, springy *skin*; and altogether it should be inquisitive, playful and alert. These, in fact, are the pointers to health you can always look for in your dog.

Take a puppy to the vet when it is nine weeks old to be inoculated against the various dog diseases like distemper and canine hepatitis. These injections are expensive (another cost factor to bear in mind) but they are necessary.

Dogs like a variety of meat, horsemeat and offal are good and all should be

lightly boiled. Half a dog's diet should comprise chopped-up vegetables (not potatoes) and greenstuff. Make sure they always have fresh water. Don't give them small, splintery bones, but they do like large, raw marrow bones. They will probably take them away and bury them if they have half a chance, bringing them back to you as 'priceless' maggoty treasures some weeks later!

It's not easy to give exact quantities of food to feed a dog; as a general rule a puppy needs about 25 grammes of food for every 400 grammes of body weight (1 oz to 1 lb) each day, and a fully grown dog needs about half that amount to every 400 grammes of weight ($\frac{1}{2}$ oz to 1 lb). A six-week-old puppy needs four small meals a day, a three-month-old puppy needs three meals, an eight-month-old puppy two meals, and from a year on they really only need one meal a day.

Your dog will need a basket with an old blanket in it for sleeping. Keep it away from draughts and wash the bedding regularly or the dog is likely to get fleas. Brush your dog vigorously for at least ten minutes a day (longer if it's a long-haired variety). You can bath it if it's very dirty, but only do so on warm days. Use a dog shampoo or mild soap and rub it hard with a rough dry towel. Take it for a walk to dry it off. The same goes if it decides to take a 'dip' in a pond or river—keep it moving till it's dry and never let it 'go to bed' still wet.

Remember that you have to buy a licence for a dog (just like the television) and this you can get from any post office. Remember, too, that it is a law that all dogs should wear a collar bearing your name and address (as the owner) when he is on a public highway.

Training a dog

As dogs are very intelligent animals, it is possible to train them in many ways. Indeed a well-trained and obedient dog is likely to be happier and a better companion than a spoilt one. Basically, obeying orders will be associated in a dog's mind with praise and reward from you, while disobedience will mean scolding, or, in extreme cases, maybe slapping.

The first training a puppy needs is house training, which is not difficult provided you are willing to devote some time to it, because dogs are naturally clean and unhappy to foul their living quarters. As soon as a puppy shows any signs of making a mess—going into corners, sniffing or squatting—quickly pick it up and take it outside. Leave it for a short while and then make a fuss of it when you let it in again. It will soon get the hang of what is expected. On walks, train your dog to use the gutter by taking it there when it shows obvious signs of slowing down. Then you won't be one of those awful people

who get dogs a bad name and make walking on pavements so unpleasant for everyone else.

In addition, you can, and should, teach your dog to sit, lie down, come to heel, halt at a kerbside and stay at a place when you tell it to. To begin with, tell it to do these things with a clear word of command, which is always the same (don't say 'come here' one moment and 'heel' the next if you want it to do the same thing), accompanied by some sort of demonstration. If you are teaching it to sit, for example, say 'sit' and push its hindquarters to the floor so it has to sit. It'll probably get up at first, so try again until it remains sitting for a little while, then praise it profusely.

Remember training will depend on the mutual confidence you have in one another. A dog is always anxious to please the master it loves. Constant persuasion with firm repetition (but *not* bullying) is the keynote to success, but never bore your dog with long training sessions. Keep calm and patient yourself and keep the sessions short, but frequent. A kind word and an occasional tit-bit will reap dividends. Bear in mind that if your dog does not respond to your orders, particularly to begin with, it's probably because it doesn't understand rather than because it is actually naughty or disobedient. Try again, patiently!

Fish

Keeping fish is not just a matter of having a solitary goldfish that swims endlessly round a small, global goldfish bowl, as is popularly imagined! In fact this is a very cruel practice, as the water surface in such bowls is too small to absorb sufficient oxygen to keep fish healthy. They also let the light in from every side, which means that fish (which have no eyelids) can never escape from the light.

Although you can keep tropical fish, such as mollies, guppies and zebra fish, it is quite complicated as you must have a thermostatically controlled heater to keep the water at a constant temperature. Begin, then, by having a cold-water tank, which is suitable for keeping many of the different kinds of goldfish.

As it is not easy to spot a 'healthy' fish from a mildly 'unhealthy' one, buy from a dealer who specialises in fish. In general, don't accept a fish that is dull or thin, or with any kind of fungus on

it, and make sure it is alert and quick moving.

Keep your fish in a rectangular tank. As a guide, a tank that measures approx. 33×30 cm (or an equivalent area) is sufficient for three 5 cm long fish. If you overcrowd the tank, your fish will not get sufficient oxygen, which will stunt their growth and make them unhealthy. Buy some sand from a pet shop, wash it several times and put it in the bottom of the tank, building it higher at the back than the front. Then put some good oxygenating plants in the tank, such as *Anacharis, Sagittaria* and *Ludwigia,* embedding them in the sand. Plants absorb impurities and oxygenate the water, so you have to change it less often. They also provide shade and shel-

ter for the fish. Keep the tank where the temperature does not vary much, but out of direct sunlight. This encourages the growth of green 'slime' and can also make the fish too hot!

If the water becomes white and cloudy, it means the oxygen content is too low. Change it one-third at a time, using fresh water of the same temperature. Put in more plants or take out some of the fish. If the cloudiness is green, it doesn't matter too much unless it is really bad. It probably means the tank is exposed to too much light, and you could help this by painting the side nearest the light source with green paint. If the cloudiness turns to yellow, change the water.

Besides any proprietary brand of fish feed, fish need

plenty of live food. You can buy water fleas at a pet shop, or cut up lean raw meat or small earthworms into tiny scraps. Don't over-feed your fish; give them only as much as they eat in three to five minutes each day, and then siphon out the remainder.

Budgerigars

Budgerigars make nice, easy-to-keep, companion-able pets, ideal for small town houses or flats. Choose one that's bright and lively, from a pet shop, or go and look at those advertised in one of the 'bird-keeping' magazines.

Keep your budgie in as large a cage as possible (available from most pet shops), preferably with a removable tray in the bottom. This makes cleaning much easier as it can be

taken out regularly. Budgies like a few toys and mirrors around to keep them amused, but don't give them those with chains as part of the construction, as they can cause damage to a bud-gie's claws. Provide at least one perch, making sure it has a diameter of not less than 1 cm.

Keep the cage out of glar-ing sunlight or draughts. Budgies don't appreciate either! Use one of the pro-prietary brands of seed mix-tures to feed your budgie, but supplement it with millet spray or wild-grass seed, green food such as cab-bage, lettuce, watercress or groundsel, and some soft fruit. Make sure there is always some fresh water available and hang up a piece of cuttlefish. Your budgie will peck at this and then its beak won't grow too long.

You could keep a male and female for breeding, but find out more about this before you do so. The wax-like skin, or cere, at the base of the beak is blue in males and brown in females. Bud-gies should not be allowed to breed in any event until they are eleven months old.

Like all other animals, budgies can get sick, and if you think yours is not well, take it to the vet in a small, ventilated cardboard box. Correct feeding and regular cleaning of the cage, however, are the surest ways of keeping your budgie healthy.

A bird left on its own for long periods may get bored or nervous and will probably start to pluck its feathers. Either get it a companion or put plenty of playthings round the cage. Perhaps move the cage near a window (not one which receives strong sunlight, though) so it can watch what's happening outside.

You can often teach bud-

gies to talk; those living on their own generally learn the quickest. Males will learn more quickly than females, and you can begin to teach them when they are six weeks old. However, don't expect them to say anything until they are about three months old. For the best results, teach them one word at a time rather than confusing them with several at a go.

If you put your finger into the cage, quietly and slowly, your budgie will soon come and perch on it. Never let a budgie out of a cage until it will sit on your finger without fear whenever it is offered.

Hamsters

Hamsters are attractive little pets, fun and fairly inexpensive to keep. They only live for about two years and must be kept on their own, as adult hamsters will fight. Choose one that has bright eyes and a good, shiny coat.

As hamsters are such active little animals, mainly in the evening and night, they need a cage that is at least 45 cm wide and 30 cm high. Metal and plastic ones are all right, but hardwood is better because it is warmer. Hamsters are adept at gnawing their way out of cages, and once free, they can slip into remarkably small places. Keep a close check on the cage, particularly if it

has any weak spots. The front can be fitted with stout 1 cm wire mesh, but as that is 'gnawable', a sheet of glass is better. Keep the whole cage out of draughts and direct sunlight, and cover the bottom with clean sawdust. Put some soft hay in one corner for bedding (you don't need to provide a separate sleeping compartment).

Clean out and replace the sawdust once a week. Hamsters, however, are scrupulously clean, and if you put a jam jar on its side in the cage with a small quantity of soiled sawdust, they will soon learn to use this as a loo. Put some small branches of pear or apple tree In the cage for the hamster to gnaw; it might just save its cage from this fate! Traditionally, hamsters like ladders and wheels to run up and down and round about, probably keeping you awake all night long!

Hamsters like a nice varied diet of wet mash (one of the finer grained puppy meals is suitable), with small pieces of meat, fish, cooked vegetables, fruit, biscuits or cereals added to it. Give only enough food for twenty-four hours, but make sure there is always some fresh food available, otherwise the hamster will get to know that its food saucer is taken away and will therefore pack its cheek pouches to guard against such a disaster! These will then soon become sore. Change the food each day, preferably when the hamster wakes up in the evening, or it will soon get stale and mouldy. There should always be fresh water available in a shallow, unspillable pot, but don't be

surprised if you never see your pet drink it.

You can pick up your pet and hold it in the palm of your hand, but beware; hamsters have no fear of heights, and may well just 'walk off' the edge. It may be rather timid when you first start to handle it, even nipping at you. As with all animals, calm, patient and gentle persistence on your part is needed to build up its confidence with you.

Common hamster illnesses are colds, enteritis and food poisoning; the last, because they tend to hide food which goes bad if you don't spot it. Look for loss of appetite, runny eyes and nose, diarrhoea and coldness of body, and take it to the vet! In cold weather a hamster may curl up into a little ball and fall into such a deep sleep you think it is dead. This is a sort of 'mini-hibernation', but if it persists for more than forty-eight hours, you should take it out of its cage and gently warm it. At this stage the hamster should wake up and behave normally.

Rabbits and Guinea Pigs
Rabbits and guinea pigs can both be kept in cages or 'hutches' out of doors, provided they have some protection from rainy and cold weather. Hutches should have two parts; one big enough for an animal to sleep in comfortably and the other bigger still for feeding and exercise. Both parts need doors so you have access for cleaning and feeding. Hutches must be draught-proof, raised from the ground and should have a watertight sloping roof. 1-cm wire mesh makes an ideal front to the hutch. Put down hay in the bedding area and sawdust in the 'living' area, and clean both out regularly.

Both these animals like bran mash, mixed corn or rolled oats as a basic diet, mixed with root vegetables. Give them lots of green vegetables—lettuce, cabbage, clover and groundsel—and

feed them once or twice a day, making sure they always have fresh water. If they are allowed to run round the garden, don't let them eat bulb plants, for two reasons. You won't be very popular with your parents, and the plants may be poisonous.

You can pick up rabbits and guinea pigs, and they will soon get to know you if you are quiet and gentle. Guinea pigs in particular are timid to begin with; pick them up carefully and hold them with both hands. Hold a rabbit's ears with one hand, to prevent it struggling, while you support its weight with the other arm and hand. Never pick up a rabbit by its ears alone.

Tortoises

Tortoises are amusing outdoor pets and can be left to roam freely if your garden has a solid fence or wall all the way round it. If not, keep the tortoise in a large wire pen with a raised waterproof shelter filled with hay for bedding. (A tortoise that has the run of the garden will find its own waterproof shelter.) Do *not* secure your tortoise by making a hole in its shell and threading a piece of string through. A tortoise's shell is living tissue, and for the same reason it

should not be varnished either.

When buying a tortoise, choose a heavy one with a good, undamaged shell, and no sign of discharge from its eyes and mouth. Don't buy

one in the winter, since this will upset its hibernation and it might die as a result.

A tortoise that roams the extent of a garden will find much of its own food, and that could include precious young plants unless you protect them! You can feed it on lettuce, cabbage, tomatoes, fruit, dandelion flowers and buttercups. There should always be fresh water available.

As autumn arrives and your tortoise becomes 'sleepy', put it in a large, ventilated, rat-proof box with thick hay or straw bedding and keep the box in a dry, cool room until it wakes up from its hibernation in March or April. Then it can be taken outside and fed. But remember it will need water before it has anything to eat.

Ponies

A group of 'domestic' animals we haven't yet mentioned are horses and ponies. Keeping a pony is something that involves much more time, space and expense than anything else so far mentioned, and you should make sure you know everything that is involved, as well as being a thoroughly proficient rider, before you attempt to do so. Ideally you should have several lessons and rides at a good riding school whilst reading and asking questions of knowledgeable people on the care of ponies.

Many riding schools encourage enthusiastic young riders to help at the schools, learning about catching ponies in the field, how to care for them in the stable, groom them, clean tack and so on, and all these things should be second nature to you before you buy a pony of your own. It is far too big a subject to go into in any sort of detail here, but lots and lots of books have been written on the subject, and you will find your local library has a good stock. Here are one or two basic tips that may help and be of general interest at this stage.

If you are going to have a pony of your own, never try to buy one by yourself. Always take an expert with you, and, if possible, get the pony for a fortnight's or month's trial before buying it. Always obtain a vet's cer-

tificate for a pony, which will say whether it is sound in leg and wind. Funnily enough, almost the most important time to get one of these is if you are buying a pony from friends, because it can be very embarrassing and unpleasant if you find there is something wrong with it later.

Before you get a pony, however, you must make sure you have a field to keep it in; in fact, ideally, you should have access to two, so you can rest one for part of the year to let the grass grow. One of them should have some sort of lean-to shed enclosed on three sides, and preferably with the open side facing a hedge or row of trees so the pony can use this for protection in cold, blowy weather, or to escape from the flies in the summer.

Check the fencing and gate to make sure they are firm, secure and 'pony-proof'. Provide a continuous source of fresh water, ideally a large galvanised tank with a ball-cock system (remember to clean this out from time to time), and check the field to make sure there are no poisonous plants and trees. Particularly lethal are yew, rhododendron, laburnum and most bulbs.

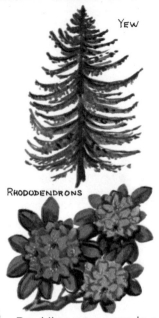

YEW

RHODODENDRONS

Providing your pony is a hardy cross-breed (and that is the sort you should be looking for) it can live out throughout the winter, as well as the summer. In winter time, when the grass is short and lacking in goodness, you will have to supplement its feeding with one or two full haynets a day and perhaps a feed of pony cubes and bran with chopped-up carrots and other root vegetables. How much food it will need will depend on the type of pony it is, the state of the field and how much work it is doing. As a general rule it is not a good idea to give grass-kept ponies oats, as these are an energy food which will make them very lively. Particularly during term-time, you are unlikely to be able to give it sufficient exercise to counteract this.

The principles of feeding horses and ponies are to give little feeds often, rather than one big feed once a day, as they have very small stomachs; to give them water before feeding (not so easy to control when they are grass-kept, but they will regulate this themselves); to use clean, fresh food and not to ride for at least an hour after a feed.

Go and see your pony each day to check it's all right and has no cuts that it's picked up round the field since your last visit. Check its shoes, to see loose nails aren't sticking into the sensitive parts of the foot or sticking out at the side where they may cause injury

to one of its other legs. Pick its feet out with a hoof pick to see there are no stones lodged which will hurt it, then walk round the field checking the fencing to make sure no one has thrown in any bottles or tins which could cause an injury.

To catch your pony in the field, walk up to it calmly but firmly. You could hide the headcollar behind your back and entice the pony with some pony nuts in a bowl if it is difficult to catch. Talk to it gently, and when you are beside it, slip the rope of the headcollar round its neck so it can't run away. Let it have a mouthful or two of the tit-bit you have brought, then buckle on its headcollar. Lead your pony by walking alongside it at its shoulder, not by attempting to drag it along behind you.

ANIMAL FACTS
Famous Film Star

Rin Tin Tin was one of the richest dogs ever! He was found by an American in 1918 in the French trenches, and taken back to the United States of America. Later he starred in several films and a famous television series, in which he performed all sorts of incredible, and often dangerous, feats.

Animal Astronauts

A dog was one of the first living beings to travel in

space. As part of the Russian space programme, the dog, a Samoyed husky bitch, began her memorable flight on November 3, 1957. During the course of the flight she reached an altitude of 1680 km. She had a variety of names, but is most usually known by the breed name, 'Laika'.

The Most Famous Pet

Probably the most famous pet in the world, and one nearly everyone knows about, is Elsa, the lioness. She was found as a cub by George Adamson, a game-reserve warden in Kenya, when both her parents had been killed. George Adamson and his wife, Joy, looked after Elsa for many years before returning her to the wild. Soon after her return she had cubs, which she used to bring to visit the Adamsons. Joy Adamson wrote a book about Elsa, called *Born Free,* which was later made into a film. It is followed by two other books, *Living Free* and *Forever Free*, which tell the story of Elsa's cubs and of her eventual death.

Oldest Animal

Tortoises are reputed to be the longest living of all animals. There is an authentic record of a tortoise living to be at least 152 years old. Its home was the Port Louis Army Garrison in Mauritius, where it was accidentally killed in 1918. There is also an unauthenticated record of an even older tortoise, originally presented by Captain Cook to the King of Tonga in 1773. When it died in 1966 it was said to be over 200 years old.

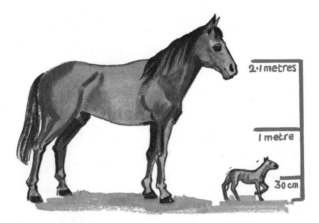

2.1 metres

1 metre

30 cm

Tall and Small Horses

The tallest horse in the world, so far, stood 21 hands high (2.1 metres), measured from the ground to the animal's withers. It lived from 1902 to 1919 and was a Percheron gelding called Dr. Le Gear. The smallest breed of horse in the world is the 'Falabella', a breed native to Argentina. They range, when fully grown, from 3 hands high (30 cm) to 10 hands high (1 metre). They are claimed to have originated from a herd of horses which became trapped in a canyon. Unable to escape, they lived on cacti, and the foals became progressively smaller as the parents were so undernourished.

Hamsters' Claim to Fame!

Golden hamsters have one of the shortest gestation periods of any mammal —just over two weeks—yet they give birth to some of the largest litters of any mammal. They may have twenty-two young at one time; just as well to remember if you are thinking of keeping hamsters as pets!

Big Ears

Rabbits are some of the most prolific breeders of all mammals. Some species can produce nine or ten litters a year, each with ten or more babies. The largest species of rabbit may measure over a metre from 'toe to toe', and the longest ears of any rabbit may measure up to 70 cm. You'd need a big hutch for them!

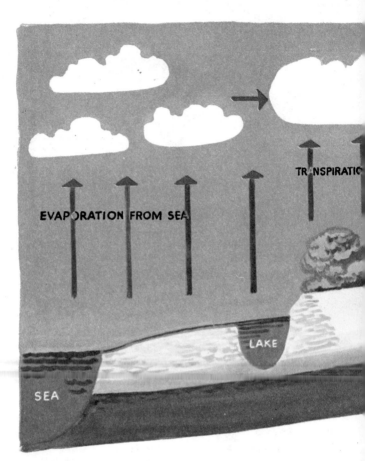

EVAPORATION FROM SEA

TRANSPIRATION

LAKE

SEA

WEATHER

The Water Cycle

All the unpleasant aspects of the weather like fog, rain, sleet, snow or thick cloud come about when the water vapour in the air condenses and becomes either liquid (to fall as rain) or solid (to fall as snow). In fact the whole 'rainy weather' pat-tern follows a cycle known as the Water Cycle of the earth.

Water vapour escapes into the atmosphere in a number of ways. There is continual evaporation from the oceans of the world, particularly in the warmer areas, and also from rivers and lakes. In addition a considerable amount of water vapour is given off from

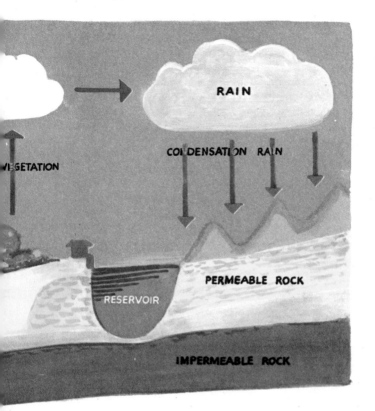

RAIN

CONDENSATION RAIN

VEGETATION

PERMEABLE ROCK

RESERVOIR

IMPERMEABLE ROCK

growing vegetation. It extracts water from the soil through its roots and takes it up through its branches or stems to its leaves, where it escapes as water vapour. This process is known as transpiration.

The water vapour is carried through the air by the winds, which take it particularly into areas directly above large land masses. Before long it is subjected to various natural cooling processes, which turn it into cloud, fog, rain, sleet or snow—depending on its height and the prevailing temperature.

At this point, of course, the water vapour usually returns to earth. In fact most of the vapour that leaves the earth returns to it in the form of rain or snow. It immediately soaks into the soil, only to leave again later through transpiration, or it falls into the rivers, lakes and oceans, from whence it will soon evaporate into vapour again. Thus the whole cycle is repeated endlessly.

Clouds

We saw in the water cycle how water vapour rises up into the atmosphere. As it does so it first becomes visible either as fog (if it rests just above the earth's surface) or as clouds in the sky (if it gets higher).

The clouds we see in the sky are composed of a mass of tiny drops of water or ice, which are carried about by continual air currents. There are all sorts of clouds—from those that look like fluffy clumps of cotton wool, floating in a 'sea' of blue, to those that fuse together to form an indeterminate grey sheet, blotting out the sky altogether. The people who predict the weather by studying cloud formations have divided them into three groups—Low, Middle and High clouds.

Low clouds occur about 2000 metres above the

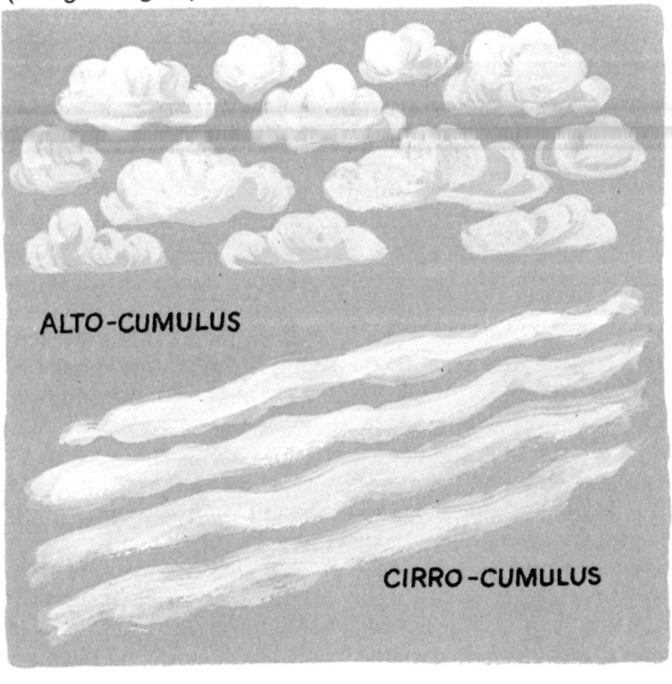

ALTO-CUMULUS

CIRRO-CUMULUS

CUMULUS

STRATO-CUMULUS

earth's surface. An example is *Cumulus,* which are the thick cotton-wool clouds, separated by patches of blue sky (unless there is a layer of cloud above them). Very often Cumulus appears in a soft, flattened form, making up a kind of patchwork layer of grey clouds. Then it is known as *Stratocumulus.*

Middle clouds are those that form between 2000 and 6000 metres. *Altocumulus* is an example, and it is a high form of Stratocumulus. It consists of near round patches of grey cloud, with white edges, and it forms into groups or lines across the sky.

High clouds occur up to 15,000 metres and are usually thin, white and feathery. A lovely example is *Cirrocumulus,* which are small, white, fluffy clouds that appear high in a blue sky in gentle, regular wave patterns.

171

ASTRONOMY

Although astronomy is one of the oldest of all sciences, until the fifteenth and early sixteenth centuries, at least, man believed that his earth was the centre of the universe, and the sun, moon and planets all revolved around it. In 1543, an astrologer of the day, Nicolaus Copernicus, produced what was a revolutionary theory for the time. It was that although the moon revolved, or orbited, around the earth, it was actually the sun which was the centre of the universe, and all the other planets, including earth, revolved around it. Not long after that it became known that the planets moved around the sun, not in circles but in near circular, or elliptical, orbits. We now know, of course, that the sun is only a tiny part of

The Solar System

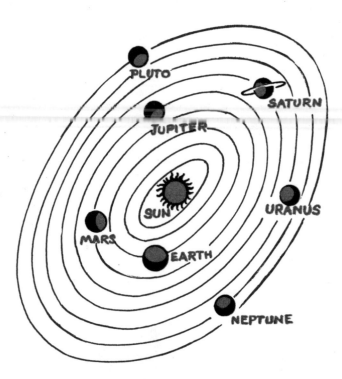

Star Constellations showing the zodiac signs

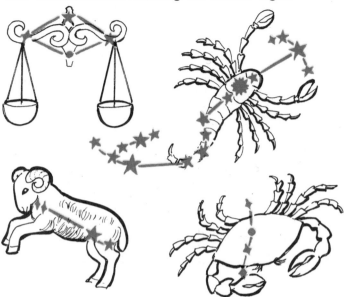

the universe and is in no way the centre of it.

Eight planets besides earth orbit the sun. Five of these are distinguishable to the naked eye from the stars in the sky by the way they change their position from night to night. The planets are called Mercury, Venus, Mars, Jupiter, Saturn, Uranus, Neptune and Pluto, and together with the sun, moon and earth, they make up the solar system.

When you look at the sky on a clear night you will see countless twinkling stars. They are actually huge spheres of glowing gas, and although they appear to be in the same position night after night, they are in fact moving. They are so far away, however, that it takes hundreds of years to register any change of position. The sun is just one of these stars, different from the others for us only because it is a million times closer to our earth.

All the planets move in the same direction and in almost the same plane. Because of this they can always be found in a narrow band of sky. The stars found within this region of sky form twelve specific groups or 'constellations', known as the signs of the zodiac.

Together, the twelve constellations and the sun, moon and planets make up the galaxy, the whole of which looks rather like a fiery Catherine wheel—except that it has a diameter of 960,000 million, million km. Even so, this is still only a minute part of the whole universe. There are millions of other galaxies, which are separated from each other by distances that are a hundred times greater than their diameter!

Some Astronomical Facts and Figures

* The earth is 148,800,000 km away from the sun
* The planet farthest away from the sun is Pluto —some 5,865,600,000 km
* The earth is 12,472 km in diameter; the moon is only 3456 km
* The sun is 1,382,400 km in diameter, and it is over a million times larger in volume than the earth
* The galaxy of the sun, moon, planets and twelve constellations rotates once every 230 million years

AND NOW TO ASTROLOGY

We saw on the previous pages that the stars formed twelve groups or constellations, known as the signs of the zodiac. The positions of the planets within the constellations at any one time have always been important to astrologers, who study them in order to understand people's characters and predict future events. But the study of astrology and the science of astronomy are two completely different things.

Astrologers study the celestial bodies to see how they affect or influence man and his environment. Astronomy, on the other hand, is the actual study of the celestial bodies in their positions in the universe.

Astrology, nevertheless, has an immediate appeal to all of us, for we were all born under one of the signs of the zodiac. Whether you are a fiery Arian, a dreamy Cancerian or a down-to-earth Taurean, it is fun to find out a little more about your own particular birth sign and those of your friends. And it is not just people whose personalities and characters are said to be affected by the stars; even countries and cities come under the influence of the zodiac signs. If you like a certain place in particular, it may be because you have a common birth sign. In addition, each sign has its own special flowers and trees, metals and precious stones, and colours.

Orchid

Aquarius—the Water-Carrier
(January 20-February 18)

Colour	—electric blue
Stone	—amethyst
Flowers	—orchid and iris
Trees	—fruit trees
Countries	—Russia and Sweden
Cities	—Hamburg and Moscow

Independence of mind and spirit characterise Aquarians. If you are happy to be on your own, studying or following ideas or pursuing causes, regardless of what other people think of them, or you, this could well be your sign. In addition you probably won't want to join popular social clubs and societies, any more than you like going to parties, or changing your mind once you have decided upon something.

Aquarians are often good artists and musicians, well suited to a lonely life in a cold garret! A career as an inventor, writer, scientist or astronomer is also suitable.

Pisces—Two Fishes
(February 19-March 20)

Colour	—sea green or lilac
Stone	—moonstone
Flower	—water lily
Tree	—willow or trees near water
Countries	—Portugal and Saharan area of North Africa
Cities	—Seville and Alexandria

Of all the signs, Pisceans tend to be the most easily influenced by other people.

Sometimes they get a bit mixed up, but they are kind and sympathetic and will often find themselves listening to other people's problems. You won't like discipline or routine very much, and you probably won't enjoy such hearty pursuits as riding horses. But you will like history lessons, because the subject excites your imagination and sense of romance.

The medical profession is a good one for you, and you excel in welfare work. Or for something quite different; the fishy Piscean apparently makes a good fishmonger!

Aries—the Ram
(March 21—April 20)

Colour	—red
Stone	—diamond
Flowers	—geranium, honeysuckle and dahlia
Trees	—any with thorns
Countries	—England and Poland
Cities	—Florence, Naples and Krakow

Are you the leader of your pack or group of friends?

Then you are probably an Arian! People follow you readily because of your enthusiasm, your sense of adventure, and because you have lots of ideas for doing exciting things. The trouble is you often find it rather boring to consider the details of your plan, so it doesn't always go quite the way you intended! Beware of always putting yourself first; it's an established Arian trait. You will probably like chunky sweaters rather than frilly blouses; steak and chips better than jelly and blancmange.

Hawthorn

Good careers for you could be as a nurse, a doctor or a dentist. Outdoor occupations suit you, too—maybe working with animals, or some sporting activity. Your pioneering don't-mind-if-I-do-take-a-chance spirit could also make you a good explorer!

Taurus—the Bull
(April 21-May 20)

Colour	—pink
Stone	—sapphire
Flowers	—foxglove, marigold and poppy
Trees	—apple and cypress
Countries	—Sweden, Iran and Switzerland
Cities	—Lucerne and Leipzig

Steady and careful; practical and reliable. That's what you are likely to be if you were born under Taurus. You may be surprised when you pass exams or tests that your cleverer friends failed. That's because Taureans plod on methodically, always getting there in the end. You may find you always seem to be helping rather than doing; moving the scenery in the play rather than acting the star role. Not that you mind this; in fact you don't often take offence, but when you do your friends will move fast, because the sparks really fly!

Taureans are good at saving money, and adding up their savings! They like

working in banks or being accountants, or just generally 'wheeling and dealing', which they do very well.

Poppy

Gemini—the Twins
(May 21-June 20)

Colour	—Yellow (usually, but it's hard to say because Geminians are notoriously contrary!)
Stone	—topaz
Flower	—lavender or lily-of-the-valley
Tree	—nut tree
Countries	—USA and Wales
Cities	—London, Melbourne and San Francisco

The sign of the twins gives a good clue to the Geminian character. It's almost like being with two people when you are with one! They are constantly changing their minds; if you were born under Gemini, you might take up hockey one week, only to drop it next week to play netball—in earnest, of course! You'll always be looking for something new; new people to talk to, new games to play. You like parties and sunshine, not being on your own or the dreary winter months.

Because of their clever and inquisitive natures, Geminians make good journalists, being happy to write about something new each week. They make good teachers and commentators, too, as well as researchers and barristers. Almost anything, in fact, if they can stick at it long enough!

Cancer—the Crab
(June 21-July 20)

Colours	—smoky greens and silver
Stones	—pearls and emeralds
Flowers	—almost any wild flower
Trees	—those rich in sap
Countries	—Holland and New Zealand
Cities	—Amsterdam, Venice and New York

The hard outer shell of the crab, protecting the softer, more vulnerable inside —that's the Cancer hallmark. Your 'hard' outside may mean you don't make friends as easily as some people, but those you do make will be friends for life. You might be a bit shy, often lost in those lovely day dreams, but you have a great ability to see things through to the end. You'll probably go for romantic books and films, and you like the sea and moonlit nights. It is said Cancerians like fruit salad and cream better than steamed pudding, but then, who doesn't?

Buttercups and daisies

Cancerians are usually fascinated by the past and have excellent memories for dates, so they make good historians and museum workers. They're good at hospital work, too, or managing hotels and restaurants.

Leo—the Lion
(July 21-August 21)

Colour — orange
Stone — ruby
Flower — sunflower
Trees — orange tree and palm tree
Countries — France, Italy and Rumania
Cities — Rome, Prague, Los Angeles and Chicago

The King, the Boss, the One-in-Charge; that's a Leo. I expect you are school captain, the lead actor in the play and organiser of everything. You might even be a little bit too pleased with yourself, ready to give advice to your friends, even when they don't want it!

The sun is Leo's ruling planet, and Leos are well known for bringing sunshine into people's lives. Your optimism and cheerfulness are great assets.

Which do you like best; large hats and Chinese food, or shapeless clothes and scrambled eggs? Most Leos plump for the first combination, but then even Leos can be contrary . . .

You'd make a good actor, youth worker, head mistress, or astrologer!

Palm trees

Virgo—the Pretty Maiden
(August 22-September 22)

Colour — navy blue or dark grey
Stone — sardonyx
Flower — forget-me-not
Tree — nut tree
Countries — Greece and Turkey
Cities — Paris, Heidelberg and Boston

Do you enjoy having hobbies? Are your exercise books neat and ordered? Do you clear up after your friends because you can't bear seeing things in a mess? Do you like doing something all the time? Sounds as if you were born under the sign of Virgo! Virgoans are the sort of people who usually keep the score at games rather than play themselves!

If you are a Virgo, you'll probably like newly baked

Forget me not

crusty bread, but you won't want to eat it with marmalade, because you don't like that.

You have all the attributes to make a really super secretary, a good statistician or a health visitor.

Libra—the Scales of Justice
(September 23-October 22)

Colour	—pale blue
Stone	—chrysolite
Flowers	—lily, or almost any blue flower
Tree	—ash
Countries	—Austria, Japan and Tibet
Cities	—Vienna, Antwerp, Lisbon and Copenhagen

True to the scales of their symbol, Librians always weigh up every situation, see arguments and problems from all sides, and have a great sense of fair play. It isn't always an advantage; sometimes you take so long to see all points of view you've missed the boat altogether! Librians' charm and easy-going nature often disguise a slight tendency to be lazy.

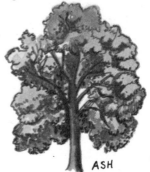

ASH

You are generally precise, neat and tidy (hate to see drooping hemlines on other people), and your creative flair and appreciation of beauty, coupled with your ability to get on with people, make you a good hairdresser, dress designer, receptionist or diplomat.

Scorpio—the Scorpion (October 23-November 22)

Colours	—crimson and maroon
Stone	—opal
Plants	—rhododendron and fuchsia
Trees	—bushy ones and blackthorn
Countries	—Norway and Spain
Cities	—Liverpool, Washington DC and New Orleans

'Never say die' is your motto if you are a Scorpion. You will live life to the full, pushing yourself, and others, to the limits. You find it hard to accept rulings from other people, but easy to disregard them yourself, and to persuade others to do so, too! You'll like heroic novels, sailing and bright clothes much more than listening to speeches on prize day or serial stories (your energy and imagination will be pursuing something else by the time the next instalment comes along).

The best career for you is one that taxes your ability to its fullest, as a psychiatrist or a detective, perhaps. Beware, though, some of the most notorious criminals have been Scorpions!

Fuchsia

Sagittarius—the Centaurian Archer (November 23-December 20)

Colour	—purple or royal blue
Stone	—topaz
Flower	—wild rose or dandelion
Trees	—mulberry, oak or birch
Countries	—Spain, Hungary and Australia
Cities	—Budapest and Toledo

Are you a bit of a tomboy? Constantly in hot water because you couldn't resist a dare? Sounds as if you might be a Sagittarian! If you are, you'll probably be fun-loving and able to fit into most situations. You could even be a bit unpredictable; so much so, you even surprise yourself at some of the scrapes you get into.

Sagittarians usually like walking, or better still, riding in the country, or feeling a sea breeze blow through their hair (they hate hats). They often enjoy exploring unknown things and usually have a flair for learning languages. Good careers are teachers and professors, lawyers and barristers. But just to show how diverse the whole thing is, they also make good horse trainers, travel agents and priests!

Silver Birch

Capricorn—the Sea-Goat (December 21-January 19)

Colour	—black or dark grey
Stone	—turquoise
Flowers	—pansy and hemlock
Trees	—pine, willow and poplar
Countries	—India and Mexico
Cities	—Oxford, Delhi and Brussels

There are two types of Capricornians—the very ambitious and the non-ambitious. If you are the ambitious type then the sky is the limit. No worry for you about keeping up with the people next door; they will be hard pushed to keep up with you. Capricornians usually achieve whatever task they set for themselves by determination, patience and a conviction that hard work is always rewarded. They even enjoy exams! Good careers are those in the Civil Service, architecture or any kind of administration.

A pastime enjoyed by many Capricornians is rock climbing. It stands to reason; why else should the symbol be a goat, of a sort at least!

Do You Know...?

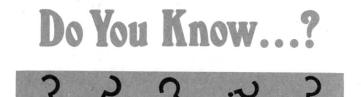

SEMAPHORE

If you are on quite a large camp site, there could be a time when knowing how to signal messages in semaphore will be useful. In this way you can communicate with people who are out of hearing. You can send semaphore messages with your arms alone or you can hold a flag in each hand.

Stand with your feet slightly apart and keep your body straight. Signal slowly and evenly, never moving on from one letter until you are sure of the position of the next one. Bring your arms down in front of you at the end of each word, and if you make a mistake at any time, signal the letter E eight times.

WHY DO WE . . . ?

Superstitions and Customs. How Did They Originate?

Blow out candles on birthday cakes?

This began with the ancient Greeks, who used to commemorate the birthday of the goddess of hunting, Artemis, by placing round honey cakes on the altars in her temples. The cakes were lit with tapers, which were thought to have some mystical significance. People believed they had the power to grant a secret wish when they were blown out.

Use X to signify a kiss?

This began in the Middle Ages, when many people were unable to write. If they had to sign something, they would put a cross on the paper. This was the sign of St. Andrew and indicated that they had signed in good faith. As a further sign of sincerity, they would then kiss the cross they had written.

Think it unlucky to open an umbrella indoors?

A long time ago 'umbrellas' were more commonly used as protection against the sun than rain. Many people also worshipped the sun in their religion, and so because the umbrella was so closely related to it, and because it also symbolised a solar wheel, it was considered a kind of sacrilege to open one in the shade.

Sweep dust inwards rather than towards the door?

This custom has sprung from an old superstition—the origins of which are not known, that associates dust with luck or money. Therefore, if you swept the dust out of the door you were sweeping the luck out of your house.

Button our clothes from left to right if we are boys, and right to left if we are girls?

This is a legacy from the times when noble ladies had maids to dress them. It was easier for the maid, facing her mistress, to button garments from right to left. Men, on the other hand, generally dressed themselves, and it was easier to do up buttons from left to right.

hamburgers; the Grand Canyon and skyscrapers. Not surprisingly, then, the largest hamburger ever made was in the States, using 'bread rolls' 4.26 metres in diameter, and the tallest inhabited building in the world is in Chicago, reaching a height of 443 metres.

France

The U.S.A. has · so many claims to fame you should have no problem in finding out some things about it. It has the longest natural bridge in the world (a sandstone arch spanning 88 metres), as well as the longest single-span bridge, and the longest steel arch. It was an American who first set foot on the moon in July, 1969, and another American who holds the record for peeling the longest unbroken strip of apple peel ever; it was 39.66 metres long! It is the land of baseball and

France is the country of high fashion, good food and wine. It is bordered by the English Channel, Belgium, Luxembourg, Germany, Switzerland, Italy, Spain, the Mediterranean Sea and the Bay of Biscay; not quite enough frontiers to compete with U.S.S.R., which has the most of any country: thirteen. France, however, has the village with the shortest place name in the world, simply Y. It also has the largest vineyard in the world and makes more wine than any other country. The French are the most active cheese-eaters in the world. In 1969 it was estimated that they ate just over 13 kg of cheese per person throughout the year, against 5 kg per person in the U.K. In spite of this, and the fact that they make 240 different varieties of cheese, they are not the world's largest producers. That is another title that may be conferred on the U.S.A., who also made the largest cheese ever; it weighed 15,190 kg.

Denmark

Denmark is one of the Scandinavian countries situated at the northern part of Europe. No point of its land is further than 80 km from one of the seas around it. Famous Danes from ages past are the Viking people who explored many parts of the world in their longboats, and Hans Christian Andersen, one of the greatest fairy-tale tellers of all time. The capital of Denmark is Copenhagen, famous for its beauty which inspired the song, 'Beautiful, beautiful Copenhagen'. Denmark has a major claim to fame in its dairy farming, which it is considered to have brought to the highest degree of mechanical perfection of any country in the world.

Australia

Did you know that in Australia people are beginning their day just as we are ending ours? This is because they are eight or nine hours in front of us in time. They have summer when we are in the depths of winter. Imagine eating Christmas dinner and sunbathing at the same time! Other amazing facts about Australia are that although it is three-quarters the size of Europe, there are fifty times less people living there altogether; it is the smallest of the five continents in the world, but looked at another way it could be described as the largest 'island' in the world.

Italy

Strangely, however, the art of cooking for which France is so famous was said to have been born in Italy during the Renaissance period. Catherine de Medici is thought to have been largely responsible for taking the art to France. Nowadays Italian cuisine is probably almost as famous, responsible as it is for such things as 'spaghetti', but it is quite different from the traditional French fare. Italy is well known for many other reasons, such as the great master artist Leonardo da Vinci, whose famous paint-

LEANING TOWER OF PIZA

ing, the Mona Lisa, is claimed as the most valuable in the world. A possibly less well-known character from Italy could be 'La Befana'. She is, in fact, Italy's counterpart of Father Christmas; she is a somewhat ugly, but very wise, little old lady, who puts gifts into shoes (another thing for which Italy is famous!) at Epiphany (6th January), each year.

Japan

Japan's total area of 370,000 square kilometres is composed of a chain of islands off the east Asian coast. The four islands, Hokkaido, Honshu, Shikoku and Kyushu, form a mountain chain which is only broken by sea. The metropolitan area of Tokyo and Yokohama has the highest population of any similar area in the world —over 14,000,000 people —although Shanghai, in China, is the most highly populated city. Japan has the largest volcanic crater in the world and has built the largest two battleships of all time, both of which were sunk in the Second World

191

War. Its national anthem is the oldest in the world, with words dating from the ninth century, as well as one of the shortest, being only four lines long.

India

India is the seventh largest country in the world, but has the second largest population—600 million to China's estimated population of over 800 million. It is the country traditionally associated with curries— lovely 'hot', spicy dishes of meat, chicken or some kinds of fish. It is eaten with rice, which is the staple diet of most Indian people, and in fact is the most important food of one-third of the world's population. For 200 years India was part of the British Empire, but became independent in 1947. It has the greatest number of dialects of any country, 845 in all, which accounts for a sixth of all the languages and dialects in the world. India has one of the most famous buildings in the world, the beautiful Taj Mahal, a memorial to 'love' built by a Mogul Emperor in the seventeenth century for his favourite wife.

THE TAJ MAHAL